HOW
TO
SAVE
MONEY

HOW
TO
SAVE
MONEY

A Guide to Spending Less
While Still Getting the Most Out of Life

ANN RUSSELL

First published in 2023 by Headline Home
an imprint of Headline Publishing Group

1

Cataloguing in Publication Data is available from the British Library

Hardback ISBN 978 1035 40595 4
eISBN 978 1035 40596 1

Copy editor: Anna Hervé
Proofreaders: Jill Cole and Nikki Sinclair
Indexer: Ruth Ellis

Designed and typeset by EM&EN
Printed and bound in Great Britain by Clays Ltd, Elcograf S.p.A.

MIX
Paper from
responsible sources
FSC® C104740
www.fsc.org

Headline's policy is to use papers that are natural, renewable and recyclable
products and made from wood grown in well-managed forests and other controlled
sources. The logging and manufacturing processes are expected to conform to
the environmental regulations of the country of origin.

HEADLINE PUBLISHING GROUP
An Hachette UK Company
Carmelite House
50 Victoria Embankment
London EC4Y 0DZ

www.headline.co.uk
www.hachette.co.uk

CONTENTS

Introduction 1

Budgeting 9

Reducing your outgoings 23

Paying off debts and building savings 49

Controlling your energy bills 55

Meal planning and cooking on a budget 105

Shopping smarter 149

DIY 183

Ways of making extra money 195

Conclusion 205

Acknowledgements 209

Index 211

INTRODUCTION

As I sit here writing this towards the end of 2022, the British are facing a bleak winter. Energy prices have shot through the roof, inflation runs riot and many people are scared to put the heating on lest they incur bills they cannot afford. I started off sharing cleaning tips on TikTok, but I am increasingly being asked if I can offer any advice on saving money during this cost-of-living crisis as well. This book, based on my own experiences and those of friends and family, is as much as I could think of, and I've tried to keep it from being too onerous. But who knows? Perhaps some suggestions will prove to be permanent? After all, who *doesn't* want to save money?

But before I begin, I want to make one thing perfectly clear: this book absolutely does not intend to play into the creeping narrative that poverty is the fault of the poor. There is, at the moment, an Oscar Wilde quote doing the rounds and I think it very apt: 'To recommend thrift to the poor is both grotesque and insulting. It is like advising a man who is starving to eat less.' There has long been this misguided idea that people who are struggling could manage perfectly well if they didn't have large televisions and drank less coffee. This is ridiculous: we are in the middle of rising inflation, a war between Ukraine and Russia has spiked fuel markets, and my opinions on the current state of government are well known. Instead, this book is designed to show ways an income can be stretched, mostly for those who have discovered that the previously adequate income they enjoyed isn't quite enough. The idea that poverty is somehow the fault of the poor has been around for hundreds of years; surely we are heartily sick of it by now? Perhaps we could recognise it for what it is, stop suggesting sackcloth and ashes for those in need of financial aid, and actually do something to improve the lives of everyone?

By the time you read this, of course, we will all know how things played out for the British winter of '22–'23, but even if everything came good and everyone stayed warm, I hope this volume will still prove useful. I cannot be alone in preferring my hard-earned cash to be spent on joyful things rather than essentials, and, with a warming planet, it behoves every one of us to be mindful of our consumption, because underpinning every single facet of our lives is *energy*.

Energy is used in the production of everything we eat, everything we wear, everything we do. It affects us all day, every day, and due to a combination of events touched on above, it's extremely expensive right now, so a huge amount of this book will revolve around using less of it. If, at a future date, the world runs entirely on renewables (and for the sake of everything that lives, I hope that time is soon), then much of this advice will be redundant. Except it won't, as no matter how we power our lives, it's certain that someone, somewhere will demand they turn a profit from it. Would you prefer your money in their pocket or yours?

The best way of saving money, of course, involves not spending the stuff, which is not all that practical or possible for most of us, and it's damn hard work for those who have the option. Living on a strict budget can also be miserable, especially if we are being tormented by adverts for desirable toys we cannot afford, all while we're slightly too cold and fed up with eating microwave pizza that cost a pound. Families on television always seem to live in such large houses (that's because of how the sets they film on have to be constructed, by the way), have such lovely furniture and such enormous fridges: envy is easy.

Above all, please be aware that we have been trained since childhood to be consumers. Shopping is nowadays considered a leisure activity, with the individual getting a lovely little hit of dopamine every time they buy a new item. Tapping your card on a terminal hardly feels like spending; money goes into your account and taps its way straight back out with no thought whatsoever. That needs to stop. Try to recognise that you are being influenced to spend – it's what our economy is based on, our spending. This also feeds into why poverty is often seen as a moral failing rather than an unfortunate circumstance often caused by sheer bad luck.

I've found that avoiding advertising as much as possible helps. I've also hidden or deleted the shopping apps on my phone – curbing that impulse as much as possible – because I'm sick of feeling mildly guilty about the unnecessary crap I have bought on impulse.

It is also worth pointing out here that my mother, who lives very remotely in the Welsh mountains, rarely gets pangs of desire for consumer goods. It's not because she is some special soul but merely because she isn't as exposed to the barrage of advertising. Adverts are obvious, though. Think about how much subtle influencing there is around you. Those people on social media are not called 'influencers' for nothing, you know, and even people who aren't actively trying to sell you something are often subtly promoting a lifestyle.

If you choose *not* to consume, or simply cannot afford it, then there should be no sense of moral failing about it. If anything, you are being ecologically mindful, part of a growing movement to try to preserve our planet. Remind yourself that your refusal to spend unnecessary money is a good and righteous thing, that you are doing your bit to protect the planet. Think about the language you use – are you *mean*? Or, alternatively, are you *frugal*? Are you *financially savvy* or are you *tight fisted*? There are so many words for being a bit short of cash and they either insinuate you are a wise and sensible person suffering a bit of a cashflow problem or are a useless pauper who consistently makes bad financial decisions. The key is to learn how and why we allow that language to be used to make us behave in certain ways, and address it at the source.

As some of you may be aware, I have spent much of my life scrabbling for sofa change, so have gained a few insights over the years, but the most important one is that you *can* have a nice standard of living on a budget. You don't have to feel deprived unless you want to – just block your mind to the onslaught of messaging that insists you define your worth by your spending power. Frugality is often a state of mind: knowing in a very profound way that mountains of crap can never make you happy, but an evening in the garden watching a sunset while weeding the runner beans can make you feel truly wonderful.

Now, I'm sure you will have heard many older people witter on of late about how cold things were when they grew up, say, and how well they managed, etc. To a degree that's true, and I will explain how people of yesteryear coped, but be aware that times change, material sciences have made breakthroughs and that the best solution to a problem in 1970 may not be the best solution today.

On a practical note, this book is divided up into chapters that you can either browse as necessary or simply refer to as and when they apply to your personal situation. While I have tried to break things down into categories, they do bleed into each other a bit – energy usage affects every area of a home, for example, so this will crop up in almost every section.

*

Before I knuckled down to write, I mentioned this project to my mother, who said, and I quote: 'The answer is brown bread is more filling, bacon offcuts go a long way, and carrots with everything. Oh, and make your own face cream.' While this may well seem a little oversimplified (even from a woman who survived on virtually no money for decades), in many ways, it is the very essence of what I expound in this book.

BUDGETING

Totting everything up

Before you can start to work out where you are best able to save money, you first need to be able to see what you are currently spending. Trust me, it's horrifying. You can write everything down by hand, but most people these days use spreadsheets or apps on their phone or computer. There are lots of useful templates that you can download for free online, but make sure they have relevant categories. There is a reason for this!

What you are going to do, you see, is go through your bank account, and your heap of receipts, and work out where every single penny is going. But – and this is key – do not add the expensive carrot-and-Wensleydale sandwich into the grocery section that you file the weekly shop into – we are getting *much* more up close and personal than that, as your different sections need to be divided further. Things such as takeaways and premade sandwiches should be listed in their own section, along with other treats, like cake, and that takeaway coffee you never get around to finishing, and there should be a section for non-edible but not strictly essential purchases too, like the lip balm you buy twice weekly because you cannot be arsed to hunt for the other 200 you have bought this year . . .

Now, bit by bit, you can start to establish what expenditure is arguably essential and non-negotiable – things like petrol, rent, utilities, food. You also need money for clothes, repairs, transport, etc. Where it gets interesting is that other stuff. Yes, you need some joy in life, but 200 lip balms aren't joyous. If you have got sufficiently up close, you should be able to see where money leaks away without it being worth it. For example, a good lunch is a necessity, but are you actually having a good lunch, or are you having an indifferent but expensive lunch, and, if so, how can you change that? Another frequent issue is subscriptions you either don't use, don't want, or had completely forgotten about. Pleasure is necessary, but I suggest utilising the Marie Kondo method when it comes to assessing your spending – look at every single item on your list: is it necessary, or just convenient? How would your life go if that thing vanished? Does that thing really contribute to your life in a meaningful way? I would rather give up my only mode of transport than my dog, but going to the pub is just expensive and rather boring most of the time, I find. Everyone has different priorities. Ask yourself if that thing is worth the money you spend on it. A useful tip is to colour code each entry – green for essentials, say, yellow for things you need to consider, red for stuff you can eliminate easily.

What to ditch and what to keep

The next step, now that you've come to grips with your spending habits, is to see how you can eliminate the red, and maybe even some of the yellow. Put all 200 lip balms in a bowl by the door with your keys, for example. Or buy one good cake a month and resolve to eat better for less. One by one, work out ways to avoid that red spending that leaches away your money, often without you realising it.

However, trying not to let yourself feel deprived is really important. Budgeting is very similar to dieting – it's easy enough to deny yourself all pleasures for a week, but it quickly becomes dispiriting, so you unthinkingly devour an entire caterpillar cake and, in one fell swoop, undo all the good you have done. Far easier to allow yourself enough pleasure and enjoyment to sate your desires – I'm starting to sound like a bad romance novel here, but I'm sure you get the gist. Some people find it helpful if they set a goal and just go all out towards it. If that's you, then find a really important goal – paying off a car loan or paying for a holiday, say – and then, every time you go to spend money, focus on the goal. Others (myself included and probably most of you) get easily distracted by so-called bargains, and little bits here and there to cheer ourselves up (and that, of course, can end up being where the majority of our money goes – those 'red' outgoings). Instead, budget for a certain amount of that and you have a much better chance of reining in your spending: once or twice a week allow yourself a bar of posh chocolate or a takeaway.*

Organising your money

I've always found it simpler to have two separate bank accounts. One into which my wages are paid that has my main expenses coming out automatically, and the second that I use day to day. Should you decide to do this too, first things first: you'll need to have tallied up your fixed expenses, as discussed. These probably don't change all that much month to month and many may well be paid by direct debit, so make a list. Things such as car insurance, rent, utilities bills, loan repayments, credit card bills, etc. Then tot up all other regular expenses. Make quite sure you include things like water bills, which often come twice yearly, and any yearly bills too. You should have most of these figures to hand already in your spreadsheet.

----

* Iceland frozen battered chicken balls are dead ringers for the ones from our local Chinese takeaway, by the way, so I just buy a pot of the sauce and some noodles – it's amazing how often there are inexpensive 'cheat' versions of treats once you start looking for them.

Getting a good deal

If you don't do so already, it is a good idea to check at regular intervals if you are getting a good deal on your utility bills. Set yourself reminders several times a year to check things such as your broadband, mobile phone deal, television package, etc. Read carefully what they are offering, check how long you are contracted to them for and don't be conned by bundles and deals that seem a bargain but contain elements you won't use yet bump up the price. Make sure you also look at separate deals rather than bundles. Very often the bundles work out as good value, but not always, so it's well worth checking. There are several well-known comparison websites available, but I suggest you use more than one, as the results you get do seem to vary. Always check for companies that you cannot switch to through these comparison websites too, as they sometimes have fantastic prices. You see, these websites are often paid commission by utility companies when they effect a switch, and you pay that commission via your bill, as it is part of the running costs of that company. Car insurance in particular is one of those expenses that it's very easy to let just roll around every year, but, again, make sure you always check. Then, if you find a better deal, ring your existing company to ask if they can beat it. Don't be afraid to haggle! In fact, haggle everywhere. My daughter used to work for a mobile phone company and, having the confidence of knowing what deals were around on broadband at the time, would spend a happy half hour beating down our broadband contract. Thanks to her efforts, we managed to beat the cheapest offer on the market at the time without changing provider.

Anyway, back to your budget. Now you've totted up your fixed outgoings, this gives you a figure you should never spend: it stays in your account to cover bills. I leave that set amount safely in that first account every month and make sure I don't have an easy way of accessing it when tempted. I then transfer the remaining balance to my everyday account and use that daily. This second amount should allow for all other spending that isn't fixed: things like food shopping, petrol and any essential expenses that are variable. Depending on your spending style and approach, this amount may or may not include more infrequent expenditure, such as haircuts, shoes, clothes, etc. But, having gone through all your recent outgoings, you should by now have a better idea of how much you want to spend on this stuff and have budgeted accordingly (having hopefully managed to whittle it down a bit).

What's left over

What you are left with at the end of all this is what you can spend, and precious little it may prove to be, but part of saving money involves living within your income. Way back in 1850, Charles Dickens wrote the following: 'Annual income twenty pounds, annual expenditure nineteen pounds nineteen and six, result happiness. Annual income twenty pounds, annual expenditure twenty pounds nought and six, result misery.' – and it's as true now as it was then (even if the figures need adjusting for inflation).

No more credit card meals! If you haven't got the cash, you cannot afford it. That credit card is for emergencies ONLY. The myriad buy now, pay later schemes that have cropped up in recent years – Klarna being one of the best known – fall into this category as well, as, despite being interest free, they can make it far too easy for you to buy things you might not be able to either afford or to justify otherwise. It is horrifying to realise how much some people owe through these schemes, but they are oh-so-temptingly accessible and essentially work on the principle of encouraging people to impulse buy and make bad financial decisions.

Loans

The only reason you should ever have a loan is for an expensive yet essential purchase – cars fall into this category, as do new roofs. And even then that loan must be affordable, *properly* affordable. Think about the amount of time you will be repaying the loan, and how stable your income is likely to be during that time. Always make sure you have wiggle room at the end of your money for unexpected expenses, or an interest rate rise. Borrow as little as possible but, equally, be sensible. It's no good borrowing £10,000 for a new roof only to have the cheap builder vanish. Make sure what you buy is reliable, as saving a few pennies can sometimes cost you pounds, as the saying goes. And do beware of so-called 'interest free cars'. In reality, you are still paying interest whatever they claim, as they charge way over the odds for the car to compensate. Check the value of the car against what they are charging. There is no such thing as a free lunch, especially with cars.

How to spend it

So, now you have your spending money, and before you decide *what* you want to spend it on, it's best to really think about *how* you want to spend it. For some people, it's easier to withdraw the cash and divide it up into days. For example, if I have £300 left for the month, I can with-draw it all in cash and then take one ten-pound note a day from the wallet. If you have money left over to carry forward at the end of the day or week or month, that's great, but if you decide you want something for £11 early on in the month, you'll need to wait until the next day, and you'll be surprised quite how often you don't in fact want it when tomorrow comes.

The other way to manage is to take that £10 note out every day, spend from it, then every evening tip the change into a pot and put tomorrow's note into your wallet. It's interesting to see what you have left at the end of the month, and you can either put that into savings, or use it for a small pleasure.

Tapping your card onto the terminal is certainly convenient, but it buffers us from the reality – it's so quick and easy that you barely notice – but counting out coins makes you very aware how little (or how much) you have left. However, our increasingly cashless society can sometimes make this approach tricky.

Make your own meal deal

This tip comes from one of my friends who has worked in catering most of her life: every Sunday she makes a weeks' worth of sandwiches,* then bags and dates them, decants juice into smaller bottles, and makes a few traybakes, flapjacks, millionaire's shortbread, fruit bars, etc. In the morning everyone goes to the fridge and selects their lunch; they each take a pack of sandwiches, a bag of crisps from the cupboard, and a bit of cake or a yoghurt, plus a small bottle of juice. Everyone puts the cost of a meal deal into a tin every day, and she buys the next week's lunch out of this tin. Then, once a

---

* If you're concerned about the bread going stale, bear in mind that those pre-packaged meal deal sandwiches aren't nearly as fresh as you think they are! Buttering the bread well helps too. I've sampled my friend's packed lunches myself and can assure you that they are great.

month, they go to the cinema on the balance that's left over, as her home-made 'meal deal' is far cheaper (and nicer) than the shop-bought version. No last-minute scrabble for change, no queueing at the nearest café at lunchtime – it's not just about saving money, but saving their time, and, as a bonus, they even get to have a small outing with the savings. That meal deal with the extra Mars bar suddenly doesn't seem such good value, not when, with a bit of forethought, you can make a sandwich at home and slide the chocolate bar out of a multipack. The £3 coffee, meanwhile, can be made at home for 30p and carried in an insulated mug.

Savings

Savings matter. Having spent many years without any money behind me, and a poor credit rating, it meant that when things like the washing machine died I was unable to replace it. At one point I had to rent a machine at £20 a month. Not perhaps the most expensive thing in the world, but far more money than I needed to spend. And if you rent and are given notice, it is horribly expensive, as you need to find money to cover your moving costs, as well as money for your new deposit, because you won't get the current deposit back immediately when you move. As the old adage goes, it's expensive being poor.

But having even just a little pot of money, if you can possibly manage it, can help with things like that and give you much-needed peace of mind. Trying to find money to save is difficult, but it is *so* important. For ideas on how to start building your savings, please refer to Chapter Three.

REDUCING YOUR OUTGOINGS

You are *not* what you buy

I need you to stand in front of a mirror, look yourself in the eye, and repeat the following: 'You have been programmed since childhood to consume. Your moral worth is not even a tiny bit connected to your ability to spend. You will not feel bad because you cannot afford, or do not want, to spend money.'

'Things' make us feel secure. We insulate ourselves from want and need by surrounding ourselves with objects; we derive pleasure from shopping and very often that shopping is pointless, done simply to fill an afternoon.

It's interesting that all the generationally wealthy people I know buy second-hand, and only shop for things they need. Not one of them regards shopping as a hobby or a leisure activity. They will happily rent clothes from dress agencies and sell things they are bored with. They buy furniture from eBay and Ikea, and always ensure they get the best value for money they possibly can. They make things last and avoid waste whenever and wherever possible. Frugality is not a sign of poverty, it's merely their wanting to make their money work so hard for them that it looks exhausted by the time it reaches the bank! It really is worth having a good think about why we demonise some behaviour when it is done by the poor out of necessity but lionise the wealthy who do exactly the same when they really don't need to. If engaging in money-saving measures makes you feel uneasy, return to the first lines of this chapter, repeat your mantra, then pretend you are very rich indeed!

That said, having banged that particular drum, I'm prepared to concede that we do need to buy *some* stuff: we live in the modern world, and very few people are truly self-sufficient. Shopping, however, has been turned into a leisure experience over the years, a fun way to fill a day buying things we don't need but which may possibly make us feel better for a short while. Social media posts bombard us with images of a perfect life we can attempt to emulate by buying a box full of cheaply produced goods imported from elsewhere and only designed to last a few months before being discarded for the next new trend. But, if you can resist this urge and stay clear of shops, you may well find you save a fortune without even trying. If you absolutely *must* go into a shop, take a list and buy only what you need. Ignore temptation! I only have to slow down as I walk past the cheese counter in Waitrose to magically buy £40 worth of cheese, so I've learned a route that avoids it entirely and walks me through the wine aisle, which is still tempting, but, for me, it's easier to abstain from impulse buys. While you are actually in a shop, school yourself to go straight to the section you need without being waylaid. Then, when you reach your area, try to ignore any goods at eye level and make sure to look both high and at floor level, as often these shelves have the items that are better value. The key thing is to learn the tricks retailers use and work out how to resist them – remember that this is an area that has billions of pounds spent on it, as every foot of shelf in any shop must earn its keep, and so companies spend a *lot* of money researching your movements inside their store and learning how the positioning of goods affects your buying and how best to manipulate you into parting with more cash than you originally intended. Avoid special offers, for example, unless they genuinely offer good value – often they just trick you into buying more of something, so take a calculator if you need to or use your phone. The trick is to stop and think; to be conscious of how you're being played.

Shopping online for food can really help prevent impulse spending and, if you pick your timeslot carefully, it can save on petrol too. Sadly, though, the discounters don't tend to deliver (or at least, they don't in my area). I also find it useful to bulk buy heavy stuff online. For example, my son drinks a daily can of energy drink, so whenever it is on offer, I bulk buy online from a wholesaler and get it delivered. It then gets stored in the shed and saves not just money but time and effort. Things like dogfood, loo roll, nappies and other awkwardly large or heavy items can also be delivered – just be sure you have space to store them.

Shopping online, however, can be just as much a minefield as shopping instore, as so much social media is really just marketing – all those perfectly accessorised homes with (oh so handy) links to the places you can buy the very same bougie trinkets, which the influencer in question was probably gifted in the first place . . . Sales very often aren't actual sales either – it's a well-known trick to advertise items for a few days at a vastly inflated price in order to claim a huge (but wholly fictitious) saving for the next month or so. If you are thinking of snagging a high-priced item in the sales, then start looking a few months before, taking a special note of prices and offers. Then you will know if something is an actual bargain or not. Beware of so-called 'special purchases' too, as they are often goods bought in specially to sell at cheap prices, but produced by brands with a reputation for quality, which is what can feel so misleading, as the 'special purchase' goods are often not the quality you would expect from that brand. Social media, of course, is riddled with 'closing down' sales from companies that are clearly not actually closing down at all. Don't bite! The algorithm is not your friend. Unsubscribe from all those marketing emails and block influencers who influence you to spend money. After all, do you really need twenty-five eyeshadow pallets? Before you scoff, I know several girls who have dozens, all bought after spending time watching influencers demonstrating them. There's a reason these influencers get sent free swag – they're excellent salespeople.

If you have an Amazon Prime membership or similar but you don't want stuff in a hurry, it's often well worth logging out of your account and seeing how much things cost without it. Remember, nothing is ever actually free – delivery costs are just rolled into the price. Heavy things are often very expensive online, in my experience. For example, soda crystals (something I'm always urging people to buy) are often about four times as expensive when bought online as when bought in the supermarket. It pays to be savvy and shop around. Get to know the value of things.

If I start to feel spendy, my trick to counteract this is to have a lovely browse on eBay, merrily putting stuff on my watch list. I then wait a few days and usually find the urge has passed. If you miss out on something, so be it. But, as an extra precaution, I did take the app off my phone, just to make it a little harder to indulge my impulses. Similarly, if your children pester for things, get them to take a picture on your phone to add to a birthday or Christmas list. Frequently they will forget all about it, or the craze will swiftly pass, but, if not, you can edit sneakily and then get them to select a few items to go on the final list issued to friends and family a few weeks prior to the big day.

Hobbies

So you've avoided the trap of treating shopping as a hobby or leisure activity. The problem is many hobbies that aren't just shopping that you can pursue instead often seem to involve massive expenditure and, er – shopping. If your goal is to save money, try to resist and seek out the less expensive options instead.

I'm a reader, so I joined my library. I can download ebooks, download audiobooks, and borrow actual books for free. If you climb, or cycle, I concede you do need stuff, but buy only what is essential, and only when you are sure you will use it. I know of more than a few men with thousands of pounds tied up in Lycra, bikes, helmets, GoPros, etc. who go out cycling a few times during the summer then leave the kit to rot over winter, or sign up to an ambitious event, nearly kill themselves, and never get on the bike again . . .

Charity shops are always a treasure trove of discarded hobbies, so it's worth checking them out before you spend your cash. I got put off tapestry after seeing how many part-worked tapestry kits came through the door. It was obvious that most people lacked the skill to make a tapestry kit look good, and I was certain I fell into that group. Likewise embroidery and quilting. Having seen so many amazing works of art produced by talented people, I became convinced I had the talent. I don't, and, I hate to say this, but you probably don't either, so start small. Some hobbies are simply good for occupying fiddly fingers: knitting and crochet can simply be a fiddle using recycled wool yarn rather than a targeted hobby. I am told knitting keeps arthritic fingers supple, but it's not for everyone, and so, before you go all out on kit, it's wise to just get a few charity-shop supplies and try it out. Either it will be a calming and soothing occupation with a nice scarf or jumper as an added bonus, or infuriating and frustrating.

Transport

It's no secret that I'm not a lover of the car, although now two of my children drive and have cars, I am perfectly happy to be driven to Lidl rather than struggle with my granny trolley. Having said that, I'm sure the exercise was beneficial. I have spent much of my life living rurally on a low income without a car. It *can* be done even if you get a bit annoyed at times, although I accept there are places I would struggle to live.

So, firstly: walk – it's good for you and good for your children. And it's free. Humans walked out from Africa and settled all over the world; we evolved as bipeds and were persistence hunters, so our bodies are built to walk. Make sure the little ones have warm waterproof clothing (second-hand is fine) and wellies for rain. It takes about 30 minutes for a ten-year-old to walk a mile and a bit, in my experience, and it won't do them any harm at all. Let them poke things with sticks and jump in puddles to make it more interesting.

If you are disabled, you get a pass on this, of course, but I see parents with mobility scooters accompanying their children to school over greater distances than parents with cars. Disabled or not, see if you can set up a walking bus if you are short of time getting them to school, then set up a rota for parents to act as marshals. Some schools are keen to help with this in order to reduce the number of cars outside every morning.

If you simply cannot manage by walking due to time constraints (children over twelve really don't need a parental escort as long as they are careful about roads), then lift share. Again, get a rota going to spread the load.

In reality, it's usually traffic that is the biggest danger for children on foot. I'm constantly amazed at the complete gridlock that happens at 3.30 every term day, with some parents parking and then walking quarter of a mile to the school gates to fetch a child in order to then drive them less than a mile. If every car had one extra set of children, however, the traffic would be cut in half, meaning the children on foot would be much safer, and it would be quicker for those in cars too, as the drop-off would be less crowded.

Interestingly, I know more people in town who walk to work than I do rurally, mainly because the traffic in towns is much heavier, so it's often quicker to walk even quite long distances. If it takes 40 minutes on the bus, 50 in the car (plus parking) or 30 minutes on foot, it makes sense to walk. Rurally, the car makes more sense, as it often is quicker (and many bus routes, etc. have been cut or are less regular than they used to be). But I think people just get into the habit of driving and so end up taking the car for what would otherwise be a 10 minute walk. Fuel has come down from the £2 a litre mark it hit earlier in 2022, but it's still expensive, so avoiding spending more than you have to on petrol is never going to be a bad thing.

I repeat: walking is good for you, and if you start walking, you may find, as an added bonus, you feel more energetic – win!

If you truly need a car, then think carefully about the journeys that you make – can any of them be made more economically on public transport instead? As I type this, a 7-day bus pass where I live is under £30, and that compares extremely favourably with driving a car into Salisbury, my nearest city, and parking. The journey takes a little longer, granted, but not much, and you can read a book and drink a coffee while you travel – neither is advised while driving! If public transport really isn't a viable option, then look at the park-and-ride schemes that many towns and cities have set up. Yes, I admit that trudging home along country roads in torrential rain can be miserable, but dress accordingly and you stay fairly dry. I might look a bit eccentric in my huge wax hat, long country boots and a man's drover's coat, but I'm warm and totally dry, so I do not care a bit!

Pedal power

I travel to and from work on my bike: it's quick and con-venient and I do on average about 5–6 miles a day. My bike is a cheap road bike and, apart from good lights and either a hi-vis or a reflective jacket and a helmet, I haven't got any expensive kit. If I wasn't so tall I would have got my bike from the recycling centre at our local rubbish tip – it's extraordinary what people throw away. Get a good lock, however. I say this because my bike was stolen last week and I've had to replace it, which was an expense I'd have preferred to avoid. This time round I have a rigid U-lock that mounts onto the frame so I don't forget it.

My fuel is sandwiches, and while at times (usually in the driving rain or a force-10 gale) I may wish desperately for a magic carpet, I know how essential it is for my well-being to be fit and healthy. As well as getting me from A to B, cycling has the added bonus of keeping me fit. It's a virtuous circle – if I do it, I continue to be able to do it. On occasion I work out how much money I would spend running a car, and ignoring the cost of lessons and actually buying the vehicle to begin with, I would need to find around two thousand pounds a year to run the damn thing. Although I would move from job to job a little faster, it really wouldn't free up enough time to pay for itself.

So, how much would you save if you kept the car for absolutely essential use? For most people, cars aren't nearly as essential as they think, they are just a convenience. But perhaps you need to see how much that convenience is costing you? Once you have a better idea of what your actual expenditure is, and how much you could save by finding alternative modes of transport, think about what else you could do with the money.

My two thousand pounds would pay for a *lot* of taxis (although taxis are rare and expensive in the country, and I'm too mean to actually use one), and a *lot* of lovely meals with good wine as well. I could even have a meal for two at the most expensive restaurant in the area with a taxi home afterwards several times a year if I wanted to, with plenty left over.

What sort of car?

It must be noted that experts recommend that you drive fuelled cars to the end of their life, because despite the gallons of fuel they burn during their lifetime, they actually had more energy expended on them during manufacture, would you believe, than after they hit the roads, which means it makes sense to stick with the petrol ones for now. However, electric cars are coming on in leaps and bounds, charging points are more accessible, and I'm certain it won't be long before they are universally available. In the meantime, if you truly need a new car, perhaps think about getting a smaller vehicle for daily use, one with a lower band of vehicle excise duty and significantly less fuel use. They are far easier to park as well and cheaper to insure. ULEZ (Ultra Low Emission Zones) are also becoming more popular with councils and a small car can often travel in them for free.

If you need a larger car for holidays or trips abroad, consider hiring one instead of running such a large car all year round. And those who live in cities could investigate car-hire clubs, but that sort of thing hasn't reached where I live yet.

Trains and coaches

Train fares can often be extortionate in this country, I'm sorry to say. If, however, you are able to be flexible and use an app to work out your tickets, it usually still makes sense financially. I can often buy tickets at half the regular price. I frequently travel to London and, while the journey is a little longer than in a car (but not necessarily if the traffic is bad), I'm generally sat there with a book and a sandwich relaxing, so I'm more than content. And, once again, there is no parking to pay. If I have a little more time, I can even get a coach, which is even cheaper than a train, and modern coaches are surprisingly comfortable. The downside of a coach is that they get caught in the traffic just as your car can, but generally they are good at factoring in any delays and will take alternative routes if necessary. Coaches may not be the best answer if you have small children, though, as they must stay sat in the seat – there is a lavatory onboard, but they cannot just get up and wander. Travel sickness can be an issue too, as they sway a bit unless on motorways, so if that affects you, make sure to take a tablet before you leave.

Holidays

We didn't. Take holidays, that is. The budget wasn't there, and I was self-employed, so rarely took time off. There are still options, though, if you don't think you can do without. The term 'staycation' is slightly annoying, but it's surprising how much you can find to do in your local area.

One of my friends does house swaps. I believe it's arranged through her church. There are various websites you can arrange it through instead, though, and you can travel abroad as well if you so wish. She blitzes the house, puts on clean sheets, leaves a list of nice things to do nearby, and then takes her children off to the other family's city – do try to swap with a family who live in a different kind of area, as it provides the change a holiday is supposed to bring. Her 'country mice' children have fun in museums and looking at urban tourist attractions, while the 'city mice' enjoy long walks and more ponies than you can shake a stick at.

There is a lot to be said for staying home, however, just spending time doing leisurely stuff you don't usually get a chance to bother with. When I lived in London, I never once went to a tourist area, as the attractions are usually overpriced and often too busy. But it's surprising what fun you can have playing tourist in your local area or off the beaten track: I'd haunt the V&A, nose around the expensive Knightsbridge shops, then set off home chuntering furiously at such excess.

The great outdoors

If staycations or house swaps aren't for you, an alternative is camping.

I hate camping.

I *really* hate camping.

However, if you enjoy such things, I am told it can be great fun. I do advise using your car if you have one, though, as a rucksack with tent and sleeping bags plus mats weighs heavy after the first platform change (please note that I'm not saying I hate camping because I have never tried it).

Anyway, I asked my siblings for some advice, as they all *do* enjoy camping and have a lot of budget-friendly experience. They might be mad (and I do often question how we can possibly be related), but they know a lot about it.

Tips re budget-friendly camping

Buy second-hand. With the increased popularity of air tents, there are loads of deals to be had on great second-hand poled tents that have only been used a few times. Look on eBay, Facebook and Facebook camping groups (Tent Talk is the biggest one). If buying second-hand, always put it up before buying to check it over. If you really want a brand-new one, look for ex-display models or last year's models for big savings.

Look for camping sites slightly outside of the more popular areas for cheaper pitch rates. PitchUp.com is great, but it never hurts to call them and book directly — you sometimes get a better price.

Team up with friends and coordinate who brings what so you don't all double up on equipment. Plan and prep meals in advance: things like bolognese you can make at home and take there frozen for a fast and easy dinner. Book a supermarket delivery to the camp site for the day you arrive to save you space in the car, and avoid the temptation of just going out to eat and drink. And it's best to remember to bring condiments so you're not buying millions of pepper mills (or do what my family do and stock up on sachets at the service stations on the way!).

Then, just buy yourself a bottle of wine and let the kids go feral in a field and give zero shits. They have fun and freedom and you don't care. Win—win, and it only cost you £5 for the bottle of wine. Remember that kids do not need constant planned entertainment. They love being left to get on with things occasionally. And even if you go with friends, children always seem to find new friends around the site too.*

Don't get carried away about electricity and other luxuries — keep it a back-to-basics adventure and look out for those pop-up sites that are often cheaper — otherwise camping becomes a longer-term investment that can be a bit like owning your own holiday home, in that there's fees involved, you've sunk too much into the kit, and you are more committed every year.

Don't be tempted to go with lots of bells and whistles. My sister always had a camping box — it had everything in it, from matches, plasters, duct tape and washing-up liquid — and it was a grab and go. Make sure you have a basic first-aid kit, though, and insect repellent too. Calpol

---

* I can vouch for letting kids go feral – I went to an overnight family party many years ago in some privately owned woods and the kids had the best time ever. Big kids looked after little kids and they curled up to sleep by a fire, all buried in heaps of coats. They've never forgotten it, and I'm pretty sure I came back with every child I left with.

for the tinies, and Gaviscon for adults. Don't forget loo roll!

Invest in sleeping bags, and a quality air bed. If the campsite allows BBQs, then it's a great way to enjoy food, with minimal washing-up, and the kids enjoy it as well.

Do your research on sites, join free groups, and always have a box with entertainment options in it in case of rain. My camping-obsessed siblings always had plasticine, water colouring books, pens, etc. on hand for their kids. You may find, in wet weather, that you gain a few random extra kids, but who cares as long as they are entertained and generally happy.

Socialising

This is always difficult when you're budget-conscious, as few of us enjoy living in isolation: as humans, we need company and social interaction. I find you try and try, and stay in for months to save the pennies, but then, suddenly, up comes a birthday. You dress up and go out, meaning only to have a couple of small drinks and be home by 10, but your resolve goes out the window by the first two drinks and you roll in at 5am, having spent every penny in your bank account. It's easily done, and the resulting guilt is terrible. Worse still, you're broke again, so you rack up the rest of the month on the credit card and, in a short while, are back where you started.

Try rethinking how you socialise; pubs and clubs are so expensive it's unreasonable to expect to mind your budget while there. 'Pre drinks' often seems like an excellent idea, but frequently you're a bottle or two down before you hit the club, and at that point you are in no fit state to make sound financial decisions. So, if you insist on clubbing, never take a card with more than you can afford to spend available, or, better yet, take a set amount of cash. Cash apps on your phone can prove dangerous, so try to move money where 'drunk you' cannot access it, i.e. keeping an account you can only access via your laptop helps – shove everything into there and have a hugely difficult password to make transferring money as difficult as possible. I have trouble entering my Apple-generated passwords sober; doing it drunk would be impossible.

If you can, maybe consider socialising in your home: invite people round for food. This works really well when you have small children, as no one has to get a sitter as they just bring the kids along. It's not a play date for kids, though – the trick is to organise sleeping arrangements for them all, let the children settle down, and then have your evening, after which the parents scoop up their offspring and get a taxi home. Or maybe, if you can find the room, they all stay over? Watch out for blood alcohol levels the following day, however.

When entertaining, the food doesn't have to be gourmet unless you enjoy proper dinner parties – a large tray of roasted veg and a chicken or sausages is fine. Make sure there's a decent pudding, though, so it feels special. My preference is for a massive chocolate cake with gallons of cream. Don't discount dinner-party food from the heyday of dinner parties either: Boeuf Bourguignon is easy to cook, heats up beautifully if there are leftovers, and easily accommodates random uninvited guests. Conversely, avoid things like chops, as if a couple of people don't show up, you'll have surplus food, and, if extra guests arrive, you end up eating an omelette while swearing blind you loathe whatever you cooked. My mother tells a tale of having dinner with a boyfriend and his family – she was an invited guest but the brother turned up at the last minute with his girlfriend. She was mystified by the chops which were served in breadcrumbs, as it turned out that the mother had only enough to cover the invited guests so had carved herself a chop-shaped chunk of bread then egg-and-breadcrumbed all of them to disguise the shortage.

If you are childless, you can just invite everyone round and get hammered for a fraction of the price of going out. But insist people get dressed up occasionally too. Partying in pyjamas is a brilliant way to go, but it's nice to push the boat out sometimes. Do be mindful of your neighbours, however, as it's unfair to inflict weekend misery without warning and, if they have a baby or are elderly, offer to help out the next weekend as penance. That said, depending on your neighbours, you could also invite them round to join in . . .

Think about daytime meet-ups in summer, as picnics in the parks are great. Have a look around for community events too – it's surprising how much fun they can be. Drinking publicly can be restricted in some places, so be aware of local bylaws (though you don't always have to have booze to have a good time), and also be alert for greedy passing Labradors stealing the sausages if you are having a picnic!

Volunteering

My other recommendation for those of you who may find yourself without much of a friendship circle for what-ever reason is one I make often: volunteer. This is my general-purpose miracle cure. It works on many levels – the main one being that it takes the pressure off for maintaining friendship, making new friends and that general slightly awkward getting-to-know-you phase. If you find a charitable organisation that needs warm and willing bodies to help, you are being useful, you are needed, they will always be glad to see you, and you should feel valued. And, best of all, you will meet other people with whom you automatically have something in common.

If you aren't the volunteering type, or you can't find something you think you will enjoy as a volunteer, then become a 'joiner'. Groups! Choirs, singing groups, amateur dramatic companies, book clubs, sewing circles, chess clubs – whatever you think you might like to try. Sometimes there may be membership fees, but they're rarely expensive. And, again, automatically having at least something in common takes the awkwardness out of meeting people, and you don't have to be an expert either. Very often the experts are only too thrilled to have a newbie to teach, and you come away with a new skill. Our local art clubs exhibit their work several times every year, selling paintings to the public, and the level of skill ranges from professional artist to keen but inept amateur dauber, so, please, join in! I have found I don't really enjoy the pub as much as I used to; it's boring unless you bump into someone you haven't seen for ages. Joining groups to do things is far more enjoyable, to my mind – you meet new people and, while some are invariably insufferable, there's usually a group you can laugh with. I'm not a fan of groups that take themselves too seriously, as I'm after the social aspect, but be aware some groups are very serious indeed, and that's perfectly understandable. If it's not for you, don't let that put you off; just move on to another group until you find people you enjoy.

PAYING OFF DEBTS AND BUILDING SAVINGS

If you are sinking under debt that you're struggling to pay off, then the first and most important thing to do is contact the debt charity StepChange.org* – they will help you set up a debt management plan and stick to it. Likewise, if you have a gambling problem, the first priority

---

* Beware of anyone who wants to charge for advice or sell you anything – there are a lot of people who prey on those in debt and only make things worse, and they often appear at the top of the Google search as they have paid to be there. StepChange is entirely free and independent.

is to get help from one of the many organisations set up to help people just like you. Please don't be ashamed to ask for help – addiction takes many forms and destroys lives – it's difficult to deal with, but you will be very glad you did. You can overcome anything with the right help.

However, assuming you are just about holding your head above water, you need to look at what money you are paying out in interest. You might have, for example, three credit cards: one at 40% APR, one at 15%, and one at 0%. Look to pay off the debt with the highest interest rate first, and pay it off as quickly as you can. If you get the chance to transfer it to a lower interest account, then do so (and don't be tempted to then start spending again). You are looking to eliminate unnecessary expenditure, and if you can eliminate high interest, you can pay off that debt a little faster.

Please always remember that your financial situation can change overnight through no fault of your own. As I type this, the pound is close to the dollar, both mortgage and loan interest rates have gone up and, suddenly, previously comfortable families are struggling. You cannot change what the Bank of England does, but you *can* try to ensure you are as resilient as is possible against adverse change. The best way is to ensure you are not paying interest on money borrowed, but do remember that 0% loan may go up without warning. But if you don't owe much, and live within your means, you are less at risk than someone in heavy debt. There are a lot of people at the moment, for example, who are struggling with the rise in the cost of their mortgage payments and I don't see it getting easier anytime soon.

Savings

As I've mentioned before, if you possibly can, do try to set aside money into savings in case of emergencies, even if it's just a small sum, which will hopefully save you from falling back on the credit card if the cat needs the vet. It's all very well working flat out to pay off the borrowings, but what happens when you have to put the debt straight back on when the car fails its MOT? Be mindful that these unexpected expenses happen more regularly than we'd like. Consider doing a 50/50 split – half in savings, half off card or loan.

If holidays are important to you and you can afford them, set aside money every month for those too, and, whatever you do, do *not* be tempted to rack up a trip to the Caribbean on the plastic. It makes much more sense to bite the bullet and miss this year in order to pay upfront next year with money you have saved. If that's not manageable either, then think about something you *can* afford.

One of my bank accounts has a 'save the change' option – every time I make a purchase it rounds the amount up to the nearest pound and saves it. I rarely notice, but it means a few pounds every month slide into savings painlessly. Likewise the change pot – find a reasonably sized jar or pot, hurl any loose change into it every night, then, once a month, convert it to notes* and pay them into your savings account.

Another effective but relatively pain-free method is to save a particular coin every time you get one. I save pretty 50p coins – the special runs with Peter Rabbit or Paddington on them. In a mere six months I have accumulated

---

* If you have a change-counting machine nearby (some larger supermarkets and shopping centres have them), it does make life easier, as high street bank branches are increasingly few and far between, but be aware that change is heavy! If you don't have a change machine nearby, things get a little trickier. The one bank in my small town will only accept up to £5 in change, and it must be pre-counted into the bags. As you can imagine, it takes hours to count out a full jar of loose coins, so for those of us without access to a machine, it's wiser to use a small jar.

£42. I'm probably never going to spend them, of course, because they are pretty, but it shows how easy it can be. If you are saving for a particular reason, £2 coins are perfect: stick them in a bottle or a piggy bank whenever you get one; the amount grows fast but £2 coins aren't so common that you save more than you keep.

There are various banking apps which help with this sort of thing too. You can set up various pots for different things and they help you to stash away money for all sorts of reasons. I've never used one myself, so cannot comment on their efficiency, but as far as I can see, the problem with all types of banking schemes is controlling yourself. You need to be able to prevent yourself from impulse spending: bad habits such as transferring the rent money into your spending account to fund a slap-up curry and another round of drinks, say. Really com-plicated passwords and accounts accessible only via a laptop might help with that, so if you are prone to poor decisions after a drink or two, give some sober thought to how you can protect yourself.

I know I maybe sound like your out-of-date grandmother, but money is really just another product. Loan companies sell money, and the interest is the cost of that money. We are all told it's wise to borrow money, to leverage assets, and in very limited and particular cases that is true. But most of the time it's just buying something we don't need. Learning the difference between a want and a need is important, and it's another thing we are trained by advertising to ignore. After all, how many times have you heard some variation on how, for example, you *need* the latest trend in coats? Do you already have a coat? Does it keep you warm and dry? If so, you do not *need* a new one.

CONTROLLING YOUR ENERGY BILLS

Saving energy – now and then

For many of us, our heating is the most significant way we use energy. Obviously, in hotter countries, it's the cooling that eats energy, but I live in England, so it's rarely hot enough to warrant air-conditioning. Our ancestors relied on wood for fuel and clever building to keep themselves comfortable, and nowadays it is possible to build houses that use little energy and can run completely on renewables (and, interestingly, they use some of the same principles used historically). Large windows with an overhang, for example, catch the low winter sun but are shielded from the high summer; equally, stone slabs that are cool in summer but warm up with the low-angled winter light. Thatched roofs are wonderfully insulating (although, if they catch fire, they will take the whole house with them – the insurance premiums must be scary), and thick cob walls and low ceilings are easier to heat. In the days before double glazing (and before glass), windows were small to keep precious heat inside. The smart Georgian houses with those large windows that let in so much wonderful light often had wooden shutters inside, which were closed to preserve heat and to provide security. The energy performance of your house or flat will depend on an awful lot: whether you have gas heating or rely on electric, how thick and insulated your walls are, the type of windows fitted and a hundred other factors beside.

Until quite recently, it was recommended you checked regularly to see if another energy provider could do you a better deal on your gas and electricity, but as things stand in the autumn of 2022, all providers are charging the maximum they can under the Ofgen price cap. This is the maximum they are allowed to charge, but at present global energy prices are so high that many energy providers are paying more for energy than they are allowed to sell it for. We are anticipating that price cap will rise considerably in the spring, so, by the time this book is released, we should have a far clearer picture of how the government will deal with this challenge, but even if prices return to more manageable levels, you may find you can cope using less energy anyway and decide to keep going with the economies you've discovered work for you. After all, there are plenty more exciting things to spend your money on than the utilities!

Keeping warm

If you are looking at improving some of the factors that play a role in how energy efficient your home is, it's important you look at how long they will take to pay for themselves. Fitting new windows to an entire house will cost many thousands but may only give savings of a few hundred a year, so obviously they will take some time to pay for themselves. Please make sure you do your sums before you lay out any money!

If it costs more than you can afford to solve a problem, you may well swap one problem for another.

The two things that always come up in discussions about energy are 1) how to trim bills and 2) whether it's cheaper to run the heating all day at a low temperature or to simply heat the house when you need it. Regarding the latter, in theory it should be cheaper just to maintain a low temperature, as the heating will never have to work flat out. Except, as ever, this isn't always the case, as it's dependant on so many other factors. In a well-insulated house with an efficient heating system, it's probably cheaper to keep things ticking over at 15–16°C and just boost a little when needed, but in a poorly insulated house, it's going to be very different, especially if the house is unoccupied for most of the day. Older-style heating controllers are not as adjustable or flexible either, so that will affect the control you have on your heat.

The very first thing to do is simply turn the temperature down. While elderly, less mobile and vulnerable people need a temperature of around 20°C, most healthy people can manage happily at 18°C, or even 16°C if you dress warmly. We have a smart meter at home (it only reads the gas rather than both, but it's still useful) and we worked out that running the central heating at 18°C for four hours a day kept the house tolerable at the lowest cost. When the temperature dips, we use heated throws and, if necessary, light the fire, which I admit is a luxury many don't have.

Heat rises, and modern homes should have a thick layer of insulation in the roof – current UK government recommendations are between 250mm and 270mm, but some new properties are going up to 300mm. If the insulation in your loft is below this, it will pay to top it up. You must ensure your loft has adequate ventilation, of course, but the rolls of rock wool insulation aren't hugely expensive and, if you dress accordingly and wear gloves, it's something you can do yourself. If you have no insulation at all to start with, it will pay for itself in just over a year.

Cavity walls, meanwhile, should also have an insulation material put into them. Some older houses aren't insulated this way, so that is something you can think about, but, again, it's expensive. Government schemes seem to pop in and out of existence, so it's always worth checking to see if any grants are available. We had ours done many years ago for free in a rented house. It made a certain amount of difference, but the floors were still draughty and the loft insulation wasn't great, which limited the improvement we felt.

Insulation under the floor, of course, is yet another aid to keeping a house warm, especially in older builds, but it usually involves taking up floorboards and, again, may well be an expensive undertaking. Many new home-owners are ripping up carpets to reveal original wooden or tile floors and are confused as to why they were covered over. The simple answer is often that the pre-vious occupants were cold – carpet is warm underfoot, and cold air can whistle up through gaps between floor-boards. In fact, that's maybe what put paid to the trend for polished floorboards during the 1970s, when, funnily enough, there was also an energy crisis.

A quick history lesson

When many of our older houses with floorboards, etc. were built, they would have been heated by a fire in each room (often burning coal, which was cheap back then), and the centre of the room was usually covered by a large rug, leaving a margin of a foot or so, and the air flowed up through the floorboards and contributed to the clean burn of the fire. Remember also how people dressed back then – long thick skirts and petticoats for women, thick trousers for men. They avoided draughts as much as possible but, between the fires, their clothing and either gas or candles to light houses, things were warm, if rather difficult for sensitive lungs. Living in one such house, where the fireplace had been removed but the chimney not blocked off, I had to buy a coffee table to use as a sort of anchor, as the wind would come up with such strength that the rug lifted and almost walked across the room! Equally, my mother's house in Wales has slate slabs laid onto the earth underneath: to insulate that kind of floor would involve shoring up the house while a digger removed a few tonnes of soil. Either that or laying insulation on top and ensuring only very short people used the downstairs.

Before we move forwards, one vital public service-style announcement: it is ESSENTIAL you have a working carbon monoxide alarm – it's a legal requirement in rented properties, but some homes are still without them. Carbon monoxide is a killer: it has no smell, and you need that alarm as sometimes ceiling draughts affect the flame of gas burners and gas fires. Do not risk your life, or your children's lives – test it weekly.

Windows

Single-glazed windows allow cold in, and old double glazing can be draughty and damp. But windows are expensive to replace and, when on a tight budget, the last thing you can afford is new windows. Thick heavy winter curtains are a huge help after dark and are often cheaply bought second-hand, but obviously you need to open them during the day or risk becoming a Morlock by spring. Finding a way to block the window off and retain the light is what you are looking for and there are several solutions.

We'll start with the most expensive option after replacing the windows entirely: sheets of clear acrylic held on by magnetic strips work well. While using the rigid sheet stuff, it's tempting to simply inset it to the wood and fix in with beading. Not a great idea, I'm afraid, because you won't have the vacuum between the glass and the sheet, so condensation is possible, even likely. You'll also want to remove it in summer to allow air in and to clean and maintain the window. However, you can get the sheets cut to size and they will last years if stored carefully when not in use. We have used this approach in the bathroom and the panel of acrylic lives behind a bookcase from May until November.

Next on the list is thick vinyl sheeting – a mid-priced alternative to acrylic, this is the heavy-duty flexible clear plastic sold by the metre. Postage is far cheaper than that for rigid sheets, but do ensure they send it in a roll, as once folded it's difficult to remove the creases. You can cut it with scissors and a few staples will hold it in place. It doesn't seal, but due to its thickness does a pretty good job of blocking the cold from creeping in – it's effectively a transparent curtain. Check the thickness before you buy, as it can be deceiving – ours is .75mm and works well. I'm not convinced thinner stuff is worth it, but you might find it easier to attach to the frame, as it's key to do so tightly to avoid draughts.

It's also possible to buy sheets of cellophane film that you attach with double-sided tape and shrink tight with a hairdryer. This works well, but only lasts one season and it can be troublesome removing the tape, but it is a lot cheaper than the previous two choices,* if maybe not massively environmentally friendly due to the waste.

Other options are sticking bubble wrap over a window, either by sticking or pinning it to the frame, or by putting it directly onto the glass using a little spray bottle of water to help stick it down. It works very well but, unsurprisingly, looks terrible. However, bubble wrap is cheap, and often can be scrounged for free. Or you could look at

---

* Just be sure that, when you take it down, you remove every trace of the double-sided tape at once, as the longer it stays in place the harder it is to remove – warming it with a hairdryer as you peel sometimes helps.

using Mylar space blankets – the silver kind – which can be effective, but neighbours might well suspect you are growing cannabis . . . Both of these options reduce the natural light quite a bit as well, which means you'll potentially use the lights a bit more. If your bulbs are LEDs that shouldn't be a problem, but incandescent bulbs are expensive to run.

Another trick that works with draughty double-glazed windows is to use tape to seal them closed. Close them as tightly as possible – make sure the frames are clean or the tape will not stick – then use something sold as draught-excluding tape to seal them up. Make sure you aren't buying the foam tape, which sits between the window and the frame – this is thick tape that goes on the inside recess and up onto the window frame itself, sealing the gap and sticking the window shut. Again, it will need removing in summer, but it can make a big difference. Just keep an eye out for condensation and wipe it up regularly.

Yet more draughts

Now the windows are less problematic, you can look at other ways to conserve that precious heat. I think it helps a lot if you focus on getting rid of any remaining draughts. An effective but probably unusual way to check for draughts is to have a shower then wander naked through your house in search of a towel, but I'd make sure the curtains are closed first.

Those somewhat twee sausage-dog things work really rather nicely – especially on interior doors – but for exterior doors a purpose-made draught strip might be better. Draught excluders can be expensive to buy, so I suggest you fashion one from two old shirt sleeves. Slide one sleeve inside the other so they're doubled up, knot one end firmly and turn the whole thing inside out. Fill with sand or simply shredded rags and tie off the other end. Sand is heavy and is a really impressive way to block draughts, and in the summer the draft excluder also works as a solid doorstop.

You may not know that UPVC doors can be adjusted to fit more snugly into their frames – it's surprising how draughty old UPVC doors and windows can be. Have a close look at them. Sometimes the locking bolts have star key recesses in them to allow them to be tightened and the hinges can usually be tweaked to make a door hang straighter. Check YouTube for videos, as it's hard to explain the procedure and I assume it's slightly different between models, but you may well discover that you can tighten your windows too. Door curtains help immeasurably as well. They can be expensive due to the size but, yet again, second-hand helps. Mine was a silk one in vomit green (consequently it sold cheaply), which I dyed black. I then sewed in a layer of something known as 'bump', a cheap thermal interlining material. It's easy to handle and you can tack it either in between a lining and the curtain or just as a lining. It's handy for all curtains and at the time of writing is under £4 a metre.

Foam insulation strip is cheap to buy, but make sure you stick it on the part of the frame that makes contact with the front of the door as the glue isn't strong. To check if you have sealed the gap, get someone to stand outside the closed door when it's dark and run the beam of a torch around the door frame – if light seeps in, you can be sure a cold draught will find its way easily.

What to heat and how

Central heating was not common when I was a child, and most households kept one living room warm with the aid of a fire of some description. The kitchen was self-heating due to the cooking, and both bedrooms and bathrooms were freezing. You do get used to it, and if your house is not excessively damp, you may well be perfectly okay if you never fire up a radiator in certain rooms all winter.

I even know several elderly people who have refused to allow the council to fit central heating as they believe it to be unhealthy.

You must have *some* heat in the house, though, even if from a small fan heater or a halogen heater next to you while you dress. Here I need to be very clear, however – do not try to heat your house with either a fan heater or a halogen heater, as it's expensive. A fan heater can take the chill off of a room fairly quickly, while a halogen heater warms you up quickly, but when they are turned off the heat dissipates quickly. Use them only for short periods of time – when you dress or undress perhaps – or just run the fan heater for five minutes once an hour. They are short-term solutions to keep you warm while dressing or when walking into an icy room. If you are trying to warm the whole house up, the central heating is the cheapest way to do it, as the heat transfers to the body of the house. The real question, of course, is do you need the whole house to be warm?

Bills

Your heating bill has very likely trebled (actually, mine has quadrupled), so that means unless you have lots of spare cash sloshing around, you can only afford a quarter of the heat you enjoyed last winter; it also appears that the direct debits being taken now are based on what you used in this period last year. Energy companies usually use historic data to work out how much you will use in any given time period, so by cutting this year's energy down low, you may hopefully get a lower direct debit next year. You can elect to pay every month (or every quarter) for what you have actually used, but be aware your unit price might be slightly higher. You also need to be completely sure you *can* pay the bill. I've heard quite a few people suggest that you just refuse to pay at all. Please DON'T do this, as repeated refusal to pay means the energy company will force you to have a pay-as-you-go meter installed. This will collect the debt weekly, and it will prioritise the debt over all else. It is also very possible that you will pay more per unit through such a meter.

From an evolutionary perspective, humans became so prolific because they conquered fire, and through this learned to free up calories by cooking food as well as keeping themselves warm. If you cannot afford any heat at all, it is ESSENTIAL you spend time in a library, or at a friend's house, just for an hour or so. There are warm banks – like food banks but for heating – setting up all over the country. Various supermarkets are doing cheap hot meals too, and suggest you can just sit in the café if you wish. Please take advantage of this if you need to. It's possible to manage with only a small heat source in one room, but you absolutely need some form of heating. Keeping your body warm all day is exhausting, and you can easily become ill. With no heat source, even if you eat well and stay active to maintain your temperature, you will be exhausted no matter what you do. You will find thinking difficult, brain fog will set in, and you will make silly avoidable mistakes – on occasion those mistakes can be fatal.

Understanding your meter

Gas can be hard to estimate in advance as it is sold by volume, but electricity is much easier and fairly accurate. Electricity is sold by the kilowatt-hour (KWh) and that, unsurprisingly, is the amount of electricity required to produce one kilowatt for an hour. All appliances will have their rating marked on them, but, as a rule, heat is expensive. Things like ovens run at 2–2.5 kilowatts, and they draw that when heating. Once they reach the set temperature, they generally turn on and off to keep the oven at temperature. Otherwise they'd overheat. Usually, they have a light that shines while heating and switches off when the temperature is reached. Things like small fans will use around 30 watts.

You will also be charged what is known as a standing charge for energy: a daily fixed rate charged for the joy of having the service to your house. If you go away and have no power in use at all, you will still pay this. However, if you know what your standing charge is, you can cost something like that small halogen heater quite accurately, so perhaps do a little working out to see if it is affordable. You can buy plug-in timers to control appliances too – many are simply clockwork and are handy even if they only act as a reminder by turning off a heater after half an hour. If you absolutely cannot face getting out of bed in a freezing bedroom, set one to turn a small heater on fifteen minutes before your alarm goes off. To be certain you don't accidentally leave it on all day, which is dangerous as well as being a waste of energy, I suggest you set the timer to also turn it off again.

Fireplaces

Many people are opening up fireplaces again and re-instating fires as a source of heating, but for a long time a log fire has been a luxury, as a load of logs has, for many years, hovered around the £100 mark. It seems that now many people are realising it could be far cheaper than running their gas heating. I am one of those people. I intend to keep the fire going all day when the temperature drops in order to keep the brickwork warm. Two things to remember here, though. Firstly, make sure the chimney is swept before you light the first fire of the season,* as a chimney fire is unpleasant and usually put out by stuffing a firehose into the chimney pot – the mess is unbelievable. With that in mind, make sure your logs are properly seasoned. Burning scraps of timber can cause your flue to get thick with soot and tar very quickly, and it's this that catches light. Fitting a log burner is an expensive enterprise – modern log stoves are regulated as to how much particulate matter they kick into the atmosphere for environmental reasons, so while you may consider this as a long-term investment, you do need to be cautious.

Secondly, *never* leave an open fire without a spark guard in front of it. This is a fine mesh screen to contain any sparks and embers that may come flying out, and, if you

---

* Your household insurance may require you to have this done by a professional, who will supply you with a certificate, a bit like when you get your boiler checked.

have children, you should have a proper safety guard too, which must always be clipped to the wall.

If you have a fireplace you are not using, however, it's a good idea to stuff an old pillow up into the back of it, as a chimney is effectively a long tube leading to the outside, so heat disappears up and out at speed. You will notice, though, that if you use the downstairs fireplace, the brick-work surrounding the flue gets warm and helps to keep upstairs rooms warm as well. Please note that I am in no way recommending those DIY terracotta heaters made with a flower pot and tea lights, as there have already been several house fires caused by these, and candles emit particulate matter too, which affects your lungs.

General principles re heating

Fundamentally, it's easier and cheaper to heat a small space than a large one. The rise of the open-plan home coincided with the advent of efficient heating. So, if you find you are faced with heating a huge space, consider how you could reduce that area. It might be you are blessed enough to have a smaller study or dining room into which you could move the sofa to over winter in a smaller but warmer room. To be honest, you might even find it's cheaper to go to bed early and snuggle under the duvet instead of lounging on the sofa. If not, then try to move the seating into a smaller area and use throws and hot water bottles to reduce the need for warmth in the whole wider area. Those large concertina screens you see sometimes were often used to confine heat from the fire to a smaller area, or to screen the door from the room so that heat would not escape when the door opened. It's not actually difficult to make a simple one: you need three equal-sized rectangular wooden frames made from wood, about six foot tall and two foot wide; hinge them together in a concertina and cover them in attractive wallpaper. You don't strictly have to use wallpaper, but fabric often isn't as draughtproof as one could wish. Either use it to divide the room to confine the heat from the fire or other heat source, or to shield you from incoming draughts. Another tip I have heard is to sit or sleep inside a sort of tent set up inside the house. It's a similar idea to having a four-poster bed with thick tapestry hangings – it certainly works, but be aware that candles and sources of ignition must be kept well away. In fact, I really think this should be an emergency sleeping arrangement only if you have no heat at all due to the potential fire risk, but perhaps in a child's bedroom it could be a fun way to get through a cold night without worrying them too much.*

Dressing for warmth

The whole purpose of all these measures we've discussed here, however, is to keep your body warm enough, so, above all else, ensure you are dressed appropriately: socks and slippers, a thick jumper or robe. Every member of my family has one of those oversized fleece hoodies for wearing inside and they work well.

Just a quick reminder: there is no point wearing a huge hoodie inside if you don't wear something on your legs and feet! All skin needs covering to keep truly toasty! For warmth in general, you are better off in wool and silk (wool especially if you are getting wet, as wool maintains its insulative properties even when damp – it's why hunters wear tweed), but wool can be itchy next to the

---

* This is important: if you have children and are struggling financially, they will absolutely know. Hiding it from them sometimes makes it worse, so explain some of the issues in as accessible a way as you can, and tell them some of your proposed solutions too, but, most of all, listen to them. It's not going to magically fix things, but alleviating their fears as much as possible will make things easier all round.

skin, so I find a vest of some description, a t-shirt, a shirt, then a jumper and a padded gilet makes a nice outdoor set of clothes. On the bottom half it is knee-length socks, long johns, then trousers, with good thick-soled shoes or boots. A silk scarf knotted around the throat to stop draughts down the neck as well. Then, of course, a warm hat and coat, with gloves or wrist warmers if it's particularly arctic.

Bed involves cosy pyjamas, with a thick dressing gown and my slippers close to the bed so I can climb straight into them as I get out from under the covers.

If you are sat down for any length of time, have a hot water bottle in your lap or train the cat to curl up on you. One of my lovely friends made me a hot water bottle pouch on a belt to tie around my middle. Strictly speaking, it is for after swimming, but it's lovely around the house. A hat inside too, if you feel the cold.

Keep rugs dotted around the place on the arms of chairs. A knee rug really keeps the legs toasty, and you can make them from old jumpers – just cut big squares or rectangles, then sew together until the desired shape and size.* No matter how you go about it, it is definitely

---

* I cover how to use every scrap of an old jumper later – see p. 192.

cheaper to keep your body warm rather than the entire house.

Do please keep an eye on your pets, though, and any frail or vulnerable people will need careful attention, especially if mobility is limited.

If your dog has very short hair, they might need a dog coat. Dogs run hotter than people, so make wonderful hot water bottles, but I suggest you don't change their diet just before a cold spell. Being woken by eye-watering dog farts is horrific . . . I mention this because, being a conscientious author, I checked out the discount online food shops I mention elsewhere in this book and bought some very expensive dog kibble at a quarter of the regular price. I'm just glad I didn't get pink eye!

Small mammals – rabbits, hamsters, etc. – need adequate food and bedding, plus lots of fresh water. Keep them in a warmer place if possible, perhaps on a table that catches the sun? Rodents do go into hibernation if it's very cold, so please check on things.

We also have several heated throws to cover ourselves and the dog with, and they are truly delightful. They are far cheaper to run than the heating – and, after all, it's when we sit down rather than move about that we get cold. I cannot count how many times we used to just click the heating on for an hour as we had all sat down to relax and suddenly become aware of the cold. No more! Once again for those at the back, it's cheaper to heat a small space than a large one, and cheaper to heat your body than a small room!

In the bedroom

You will find you sleep extremely well in a cold bedroom if the bed itself is warm. Hot water bottles or electric blankets mean you get into a warm bed, which is lovely, but do NOT leave an electric blanket on once you are in the bed. On a basic level, it will disturb your sleep, as it can cause over-heating in some people, but, for the unlucky few, they can catch fire. A caveat with hot water bottles too – check they are in good condition if they have been in storage, as rubber does perish and you don't want to be scalded.

Many older people will remember dressing in front of a downstairs fire on chilly mornings, and ice on the inside of the bedroom window was once a common occurrence. Away at school, we had a sink in our mostly unheated dormitory that frequently froze in winter, and we had no warm kitchen in which to dress – it was up and into clothes as fast as possible. Interestingly, ex-boarding school pupils seem to fall into the two extremes. We either abhor the slightest trace of a draught and need to have a warmed bed (my camp) or we sleep with the window open all year round, prefer icy-cool sheets and cannot sleep with the heating on.

I was luckier at home, though, as my grandmother kept a paraffin stove alight in the kitchen all winter, so our kitchen was toasty warm and fuggy. A huge kettle lived on top to supply a constant source of hot water for washing and endless cups of tea.

Paraffin heaters have now gone the way of the dodo and, to be honest, that is a good thing. They pushed out an incredible amount of moisture into the air, were a massive fire risk and, if the wick was not carefully monitored, they could give off carbon monoxide. This point is made to illustrate that not all old-fashioned solutions are the best ones.

I still find the distinctive smell comforting, though.

Air flow and avoiding damp

The windows of an unheated bedroom will need opening in the morning, and often need wiping of the condensation that builds up overnight. I also advise pulling furniture away from the walls by several inches to allow air to circulate. My bed sits against an outside wall, which is extremely cold, so I've put a sheet of stiff foil insulation between the bed and the wall. It's loose, so avoids mould growing – mould is something you really need to keep an eye out for. Ventilation really matters in a cooler house, as humans give off moisture every time we breathe. In fact, it's estimated that healthy adults may exhale around one litre of water every night.[*] In your efforts to keep the cold out and the warmth in, don't overlook the importance of ventilation and air flow.

If your budget allows, a desiccant dehumidifier can be a good investment. After the initial outlay, it should pay for itself within a few years. They blow out a stream of warm dry air – I used ours instead of the storage heater in a very cold and damp bedroom for several years and it was never cold, so they double as a heat source.

Condenser dehumidifiers have come along in leaps and bounds too, so if you need one to remove serious damp, and are operating at above around 15°C, you can now buy small quiet ones that run at about 50db (roughly the same as a fridge, I gather), and they work out a little

---

[*] https://www.solihullcommunityhousing.org.uk/images/stories/fleximedia/condensation-leaflet.pdf

cheaper than the desiccant ones to buy. However, as with all appliances, sit down with a calculator and read reviews.

If you've not got a dehumidifier, then be punctilious about opening windows when it is dry: ventilation helps prevent the cold, damp and mouldy conditions that are so hazardous to health. Look to see if your windows have trickle vents – they look like a sort of slidey thing set into the frame at the top and they allow a trickle of air to flow through. Open them and, if they look clogged with cobwebs, run a small brush through to clean them out.*

Types of damp

Don't forget there are two types of damp: that which comes from outside, and that which comes from inside. As I mentioned earlier, it is impossible to prevent damp from the inside as humans let out moisture with every breath, then cooking, washing and bathing produce even

---

* I have seen ideas for addressing damp – such as using bags of salt or of cat litter – shared online and, yes, they will absorb moisture from the air, but you must replace them once they are damp, so they may work out pricier than you think, and you also have to dispose of them. I can't imagine they are terribly efficient in larger spaces either.

more. You can help to ensure it doesn't accumulate too much, however, by making sure you ventilate properly, wipe condensation off windows and just keep an eye on things. The other type should not be a problem in a solid well-built house, but in substandard housing it can be horrendous. Gutters need to be clear and drain freely, the roof should not leak, windows should fit snugly, and the interior walls should be dry. Make sure airbricks are not obstructed and that the damp-proof course (looks like a line of black tar-like stuff a few inches above ground level on the outside walls) has not been bridged. If you rent and it appears you have damp, then contact your land-lord – if they are unwilling to help, then ring your local council for advice. You have rights in law and sometimes you may need a little help to assert those rights. Sadly, much social housing is in a terrible state of repair, as aus-terity has cut public spending so much that councils are avoiding as much work as possible. If you rent privately, the council may be willing to offer advice, but I also suggest you contact Shelter, a housing charity, for help. I have seen more than a few houses where so-called damp specialists have dismissed obvious water ingress as just down to people not ventilating. It's worth asking more than one specialist, as sometimes a good builder can be more help than the supposed expert. First, though, make sure outside damp isn't creeping in through your walls or your roof; make sure gutters aren't blocked and windowsills are doing their job. Go up into the roof space (carefully, though – only put weight on joists) and see what is happening in the hidden bits.

The age of the house will affect the solution to damp: modern buildings need modern solutions, but transfer those solutions to a historic house and you risk the problem getting worse. Things like cement render used to be put onto old houses to protect against damp, but can actually make things worse, as it prevents older, softer brick from drying out. If you look at the pointing (that's the line of cement between bricks) and it is sticking out from worn soft brick, you may need to rake it all out and repoint with lime, which allows the house to 'breathe' in a way modern cement render, etc. doesn't. There is a house nearby that for many years had cement render and metal window frames, and it always looked tatty and damp, but the new owners stripped off the render, used lime mortar to repoint and used lime plaster inside, then put wood windows in. Apart from looking much smarter, it is apparently perfectly dry, but it can't have been cheap. You do have to play detective at times, and as I have mentioned, you should never rely on just one opinion, especially with older houses, as old buildings need careful handling. But I firmly believe that when the more traditional building methods are employed, they can be as dry and draught-free as a modern new build.

Mould and mildew

In general, air needs to be able to circulate around furniture, so pull things like wardrobes and sofas away from the wall every so often to check everything is okay behind. If you see signs of mould, then wash down the wall and leave whatever it was pulled out away from the wall until spring. Until you change the conditions under which it grows, mould will return. Sometimes, though, very small changes in airflow are enough to prevent a reappearance.

Regarding mould and mildew, always remember it's from the fungi family, and that mould spores are incredibly common. In fact, they are in every breath we take. Certain moulds in concentration are hazardous to human health, however – they affect our breathing – so while it's not worth worrying too much about the occasional dusting of mould around a window (just wipe it off), it *is* worth understanding it a bit. The majority of any fungus is generally hidden – the mycelium burrow in soil, wood, walls, etc. and need damp to thrive. The bit you see is the fruiting body, and that ripens and produces spores. It's the spores that cause us harm. You can buy various mould-killer sprays, mould-killing paint, etc., and these are very effective. Bleach also kills mould effectively, but it must be left to soak in in order to kill the mycelium or the visible part will swiftly grow back. As a rule, all of the mould killers ask you to wash the visible mould off, then you spray on the solution and leave it to dry. However, even if you kill all the mould, you will soon get more growing back unless you change the conditions.

If you still have issues, you can use something called 'positive input ventilation' – it's basically a small unit that pushes dry air from inside your roof into the house, and it makes the air pressure inside fractionally higher than that outside and keeps things dry. The units cost several hundred pounds, but, if you own your own home, may prove a wise investment.

Then there are the dehumidifiers we've already discussed, which you can take with you if you rent your home. If all that is beyond your means, then try to get air moving around: leave the bathroom door open when it's not in use, use a fan to create air currents, and, as I've said, pull furniture away from walls. Just leaving shower doors open, and the bathroom door open too, can often work wonders.

General household hygiene

Simply put, and to return to the topic of my first book, you don't need a mountain of expensive branded products to maintain a clean and pleasant home. This is similar to personal hygiene; your home does not have to smell of synthetic fragrance and detergents to be clean. Rather than expensive shop-bought ones, old t-shirts and cotton shirts make excellent cleaning cloths, cut into squares and stored in an old bag ready for use. You'll be surprised what you can clean with a cloth and hot soapy water, and many of the expensive sprays can be refilled with water and a drop or two of washing-up liquid – frankly, it's the soaking rather than the ingredients that make most sprays so effective. A squeegee to remove water from glass removes the need for glass cleaner, and if you remember to use it after a bath or a shower, it cuts down how often you need to clean as well.

A few things do make life easier, however – oven cleaners and limescale-removing sprays do jobs hot soapy water struggles with, but if you wipe the oven after every use, and squeegee the shower screen, the frequency with which you need to use these products is massively reduced. Little and often is always a good idea when it comes to housework.

I've seen various home-made concoctions for cleaning touted here and there and some of them work, but some are not worth the time. The only one I have had vouched for uses conkers (called 'buck eyes' in the US) – you gather them, chop them as fine as possible while still fresh, then lay them out to dry. Once properly dried out, the chopped-up pieces can be stored in jars, then a spoonful is soaked in hot water, with the resulting liquid used as a detergent. I have friends who have used this for years, and I've never noticed them looking dirty in the slightest – I gather they use this solution for both laundry and floors! These same friends have also reported back that they had tried several of the other 'natural' detergents that regularly get recommended, including ivy leaves, and found them lacking. Soap nuts – literally a type of nut from a tree native to southern India, which contains saponin, a natural detergent – work, but are expensive.

White vinegar is useful and, if bought in 5-litre containers, is cheap: I use it as a mild anti-bac solution and for furniture polish. It's an excellent replacement for fabric softener too, but it's not strong enough to clear limescale in my area, even though it will work in areas where the water is not so hard. Bicarbonate of soda is a handy, mildly alkaline powder, which can be used as a very gentle scouring paste when mixed with a smidgen of water.

The problem with some of these ideas, however, is that they might be eco-friendly but often they aren't truly budget friendly, and can sometimes be less efficient, so do be aware of the downsides. We are aiming to save money but live well. Using lemons, for example: they're lovely in food, but at 40p a lemon, they are much more expensive than vinegar and, when used for cleaning, can leave things rather sticky if you don't rinse properly. Much nicer to use them in gin than in your kettle!

Cleaning clothes

Clothes need to be clean, but not every piece of clothing needs washing after every single wear. Underwear and socks are essential, and shirts probably too, but it depends if you sweat or not. If you just put a shirt on and swapped it out a few hours later, you can very likely put it on a hanger for a second wear; trousers and skirts usually just need a quick shake and hanging. If you work in an office environment, you can avoid looking the same each day by wearing, for example, a skirt on Monday, Wednesday and Friday, and trousers on the Tuesday and Thursday, swapping items around so everything gets worn several times but never repeating the outfit completely. If you do this, make sure you sponge off small marks every time you take them off and give them a good shake. Perhaps a touch of an iron to smooth out any creases too? I know trouser presses are outmoded, but if you wear tailored trousers at work and see one second-hand for a few pounds, grab it! They really do keep trousers looking smart all week for little to no effort. On that note, if tailoring at work is essential, please ensure you buy two pairs of trousers or skirts to each jacket – it's well worth it. And keep an eye out for small holes or tears – catch them early and a few stitches will return the garment to good order; leave it too long and you may have to discard a nice piece of clothing.

If you are likely to put natural fabrics such as wool and silk back into the drawer without washing, it is wise to have a few mothballs in the drawer, as moths are apparently attracted to the residue we leave on clothes, and finding your drawer of lovely jumpers are full of moth holes is upsetting. There are now very efficient moth balls that do not smell overly strongly of naptha, so track some of those down. Lavender bags and cedar balls smell lovely, but I've never found them terribly efficient at stopping moths from chewing my clothes. Wool, interestingly, doesn't need washing very often at all, as it has naturally stain-resistant qualities – sponge off any marks and hang to air. It's naturally anti-bacterial, so if it looks clean, and smells okay, then keep wearing it!

When washing, try to keep the temperature as low as possible – firstly to save energy, but also because items washed cool fade less readily. Modern detergents are designed to work well at very low temperatures, so most of our washing at home is done on 20°C and, so far, we have had excellent results. Be sparing with detergents too, as it's unlikely you will need more than a spoonful of detergent in a machine: read the instructions on the packet, and if you live (as I do) in a hard water area, put a spoon of soda crystals into the machine and the smallest amount of detergent they suggest. For lightly worn clothes, you may not need any detergent at all. I always used to wash pure white on a very hot wash, firstly to be certain they gleamed, but also to keep the machine clean. However, since the price rises, I have been turning down the temperature to 20°C, 30°C at the maximum, and haven't noticed any difference. What I do now is use washing machine cleaner once a month, and I am very careful indeed not to overdose the detergent, so as not to waste it but also to keep the machine running efficiently. To ensure the pipes stay extra clean, I am only putting detergent into the drum – I have saved lots of those little silicon dosing balls that came free with the liquid stuff specifically for this.

I rarely use fabric softener, as I'm not a fan of that chemical laundry smell, and it will make clothes feel greasy if you overuse it. It can also make them smell sour if it builds up, and you may well find you don't miss it at all if you stop using it (and you should never use it for towels anyway). I mentioned earlier that white vinegar works well as a replacement, but you only need a little – only just fill the reservoir for conditioner. I think it works by slightly softening the water, so that it rinses better, but there is some suggestion it degrades the seals, so use with caution.

Most importantly, keep the tumble dryer, if you have one, only for absolute emergencies, as even the modern energy-efficient ones use up a lot of energy. You can still dry outside in winter; your clothes may take a bit longer, but if the pavements are dry, your clothes should dry too. If it's not too windy, you can even put your gazebo up over a rotary washing line to keep the rain off. Or do what one friend does and have a washing line in the green house. If none of this is viable, hang your clothes inside on an airing rack (don't heap them up or they won't dry – spread them out thinly so the air can circulate) and play a fan on them to create an indoor breeze to aid drying. Make sure you leave windows ajar, though, to avoid it getting damp inside as the wetness evaporates.

Heavier things such as dresses or jumpers can be put on hangers and hooked onto door frames – just make sure with jumpers that they aren't pulling out of shape.

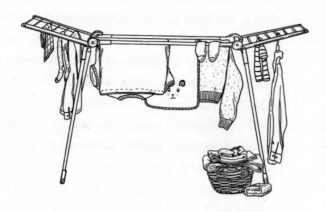

Long things, meanwhile, such as duvet covers, can be hung flat over doors, as long as you put a bin liner over the door first to stop the damp getting into the door, and to protect the clean cover from any unseen dirt atop the door.

In my house we find it's better to do a small cold wash daily and hang clothes at once, as it avoids having too many things hanging around. And I have bought a heated airer, which works fairly well, but we found that if you put a sheet over the whole thing it's more efficient, as it retains the heat. Some models even come with fabric covers that zip up that replicate the same effect.

While some expenditure is worthwhile, some may not be worth it for you. I already had a dehumidifier, and if I had to choose between a dehumidifier and a heated airer, I would choose the dehumidifier. My heated airer was expensive, but I think it will pay for itself within the year – it's not as convenient as the tumble dryer, of course, but so *very* much cheaper to run at 200w vs 3kw!

However, as we've already touched on, drying washing inside puts more moisture into the air, so ventilation is essential.

'A good blast through'

A rather useful habit I got into years ago was 'a good blast through'. I know it might feel counterintuitive when you've been doing so much to keep the warm in and draughts out, but, once a day, open doors and windows to let a really good flow of air through the whole house. It replaces the stale air, freshens things up nicely, and, unless it's pouring with rain, is generally an excellent idea. Sadly, some houses don't have a good airflow through them, so you may need to use fans to help the sluggish air move up and through, or maybe stand and flap the front door like an oversized fan. Who cares what the neighbours think!

Cleaning yourself

If you live in a hot country and sweat copiously, you will need to shower often; if you live in a cold climate and rarely break a sweat, you don't.

Despite various rather odd takes, it has never been socially acceptable to smell; it is merely that different climates and cultures had different ideas of what clean smelt like and differing ways of cleaning themselves.

Bathing, steaming, and oiling and scraping were common in the ancient world. Then, with the advent of the plague, much of Europe felt that opening the pores in warm water was injurious; they changed their close linen underwear daily but rarely bathed their entire body. My grandmother's generation bathed weekly or monthly, washing the essentials while standing up in between to be economical with water and heat. Those who did dirty jobs bathed daily, however, often in tin baths set in front of the fire. Modern-day Americans have been known to shower twice daily, using perfumed deodorants so liberally they can be smelled from a distance.*

All this is to illustrate that it is perfectly possible to be clean, and healthy, without using vast amounts of energy. But whether you prefer a bath or a shower, your personal hygiene routine uses both water and energy. Showering is certainly cheaper than bathing, but heating water does use quite a bit of energy, no matter how you apply it to your skin. I doubt many of us truly enjoy the idea of cold showers (invigorating and healthy though they might be). But I personally cannot bear showers in winter, as I

---

* My lovely editor pointed out how very unfair to Americans this comment was, so I must concede that a wall of Lynx Africa often signals mating season in British youth, so it's far from a US-only thing.

always feel that bits of wet skin that aren't entirely under the shower head get chilled, making the whole experience far too cold and miserable for my liking, so I'd need to heat the bathroom to a far higher temperature than I can afford to compensate. Baths are my preferred choice during the winter months, as I can soak for a while, warm up nicely, then dive into a warm bed, but baths are costly, as it takes a lot of energy to heat up the water for a full bath. According to Moneystepper.com, a 150-litre bath costs between 30p to 90p, whereas an eight-minute shower costs between 20p to 30p.*

Sharing a bath to save both water and energy, meanwhile, is far less romantic than you'd think: one of you always gets the tap end and any attempt at intimacy involves water getting everywhere. It does, however, save quite a bit of energy, so if you choose your bathing partner carefully, it's not such a bad idea. Much the same goes for showering together, but be careful you don't end up red faced in A&E after getting ideas about shampoo bottles! You could, of course, hop in the bath one after another, as used to be done in days gone by, letting the cleaner person go first – that might lead to arguments,

---

* https://moneystepper.com/save-money/cost-to-run-a-bath-or-have-a-shower/

but is certainly more comfortable. Top up with some hot water, though, as it's surprising how quickly water cools.[*] Also make sure that the first bather doesn't shave in the bath – no one wants all those little hairs floating in the water!

Many people suggest showering at the gym, but, honestly, gym membership is expensive and, financially, you'd potentially be better off showering at home and cancelling gym membership entirely. It is perfectly possible to exercise outside of a gym, after all, and it seems quite a few people pay monthly for membership and attend rarely. Obviously, if you actually benefit from and use your gym membership, then certainly pass on the cost of hot water to them, but I know more people who rarely use the gym than those who use it daily.

If reducing those energy bills is crucial, and you don't fancy the icy plunge, then introduce yourself to the strip wash. Here's how, for a generation who might not be familiar with the mechanics of it:

---

[*] If you have a boxed-in rather than freestanding tub, it can be worth taking the panels off and putting some extra insulation around the base of the bath – just make sure the pipes are accessible for plumbing emergencies.

Strip wash — how to

Fill the basin with hot water and have two flannels at hand, plus a bar of soap and two towels.

First: wash your face and neck using flannel no. 1, blot dry and move on to your armpits. Lather up and rinse off over the sink, then dry off.

Wring out flannel no. 1 and hang to air and move on to flannel no. 2. This washes your undercarriage, being wary of where the soap goes if you are female. Rinse, and dry with the second towel, then feet get washed. Flannel no. 2 goes in the laundry and flannel no. 1 is relegated to flannel no. 2 the next day.

This old-school method of washing renders you clean and sweet smelling while only using about 5 litres of water. Then you can relegate the bath or shower to a once- or twice-weekly event. If you have dry skin, you may find this routine improves its condition, as we all have a natural biome that protects us from the elements and too-frequent or aggressive washing can disrupt this. It's also not unknown for people to find they smell less (although not always, so please be mindful).

The reason for this is kind of interesting. As mentioned, we are all coated with a microbiome that helps keep our skin in good condition. In fact, it gives us each our unique smell, which is why people have often noticed that when they switch to a new sleeping partner their own odour changes. That is because sleeping partners share bacteria, and bacteria contribute to your unique body odour. It may sound a bit grim, but those bacteria munch away at the debris from our skin and what they excrete can smell, and that smell varies with the bacteria. In some unlucky individuals, antiperspirant use can lead to an increase in smell rather than the hoped-for decrease. Studies into our exterior and interior microbiome are still in their infancy, but it certainly seems we owe a lot to the colonies of bacteria we host throughout our lives.

The only part of your body you *must* wash multiple times daily is your hands. Use soap and lather every inch up to your wrists – it always surprises me when people shower twice a day but never wash their hands.

As for hair, I wash mine once a week and always have done. I simply lather it up, rinse off and I'm done, but I do brush properly to ensure dust is removed and any oil produced by my scalp is smoothed down the hair shaft to protect it. I suspect that if you use a lot of products you maybe need to wash your hair a bit more, but remember: do what works for you. Once again, companies who make hair products want you to buy lots and lots of it and so aim to get you to wash your hair daily! Personally, I lather up with whatever comes to hand, and I have found the bars of solid shampoo very effective, plus they last for ages. My daughter, however, has expensively coloured hair and uses exceedingly expensive shampoo to prolong the colour she paid so much for, and in her circumstance it's the economic option (she worked it out after I nearly fainted at the price of the stuff). As ever, it's not an economy if it costs you more in the long run – there's no point paying a fortune at the hairdresser and then ruining all their hard work.

Synthetic detergents rinse far more easily than soap and can be less drying to both our skin and hair, which has made hair washing far quicker and easier. Now we can wash it more often, we do, but hair can be healthy and clean without such regular washing. It's hard to imagine life before the synthetics were common, but plain old soap was prevalent until at least the middle of the twentieth century. Germany produced the first synthetic detergent in the First World War, and prior to that women relied on just soap to wash everything that couldn't be washed with lye or washing soda – dishes, people, hair, you name it.

You see, there is a reason women always used washing their hair as an excuse to get out of evening activities: hair washing took time, soap was hard to rinse out, and conditioner wasn't yet a thing, so combing out and drying your mane in front of the fire took hours. Then it needed setting on rollers or pinning up into a bun. It wasn't done daily, but often only once a month; meticulous brushing kept it shining in between washes. If you look at pictures of women prior to the war, they have lovely hair: beautifully shining and apparently very healthy.

Bar soap works out far cheaper than liquid detergent, I find, but in hard water areas it does tend to produce a sticky scum that produces that grubby ring around the bath. It's why bath salts originally became so popular, as they softened the water to allow the soap to produce a luxurious foam in the days before liquid soap was available. If you do use bar soap still, I suggest you unwrap it and store in a drawer with your clothes for some months, as not only does it gently perfume your clothes but it also dries out slightly and so lasts much longer. When you only have a sliver left, save it. You can either make soap jelly for washing delicates, or buy one of those small jute bags for scraps. For the latter option, you fill the bag and use it instead of a sponge to exfoliate and clean your skin using the very last bit of the soap. The jelly, meanwhile, is made by crumbling leftover soap into a jar, adding a little boiling water and leaving it to melt, shaking it every so often. The resulting jelly works to clean woollens and delicates, but if left too long can go mouldy (and always use a little washing soda with it to avoid the dreaded soap scum in hard water).

When I was a child, a popular DIY gift for one's mother was a jar of soda crystals, with a drop of food colouring and squirt of her scent (taken without knowledge), shaken together to make them prettily coloured and attractive. A handful of these would be thrown in the bath to soften the water. Those crystals were large soapy lumps, whereas today soda crystals are more like a fine powder – I wondered why? I also wondered if they could still be used in the bath, as modern bath salts are either Epsom salts (magnesium sulphate) or just salt (Sodium Chloride).

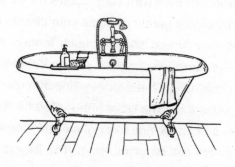

It turns out they are the same chemical (Sodium Carbonate), but they used to be produced by growing the crystals, a process that took seven days. Today they are forced with a vacuum and the process takes only 40 minutes. If you fancy a project for children, you can dissolve the powdery fine crystals in boiling water and leave the solution to evaporate slowly and see what happens. Many of you will have grown crystals in science classes at school, and easy science projects at home are a great way to engage children with basic chemistry. You can still use the fine powdery soda crystals in the bath too – it is suggested that around 100g to a full bath is about right, but I'd start with a bit less and see how it goes. In hard water areas it's worth putting a spoonful into the bath before adding bubble bath, as it makes the stuff go much further, but be sparing with bubble bath in softer water.

Toothpaste advertising always shows the actors squeezing a rather generous line of paste on the brush, and if you read the small print on the packaging, it suggests a pea-sized dab for children. The implication, of course, is that adults need more: the visual on the box gives you the clue. In actual fact, if you look at independent sources online, you will discover that it's *adults* who need only a pea-sized dab and children much less. Once again, you are being influenced (ever so subtly) to use far more product than you need. I know this sounds penny pinch-ing, and it is, but those pennies add up. And why waste anything unnecessarily? In the UK, we use 300 million tubes of toothpaste a year,* and if we all use twice as much as is recommended, that equates to 150 million tubes going to waste. That waste costs money to remove from wastewater, costs energy to produce, and costs energy to transport, so while individually it may seem trivial, it really isn't when you look at the country as a whole.

You will note an ongoing theme here that we've touched on before: being persuaded to use far more of products than is necessary, so always think about how much prod-uct you truly require, as it's highly likely you are using far more than needed.

---

* '300 million toothpaste tubes go to landfill', *British Dental Journal*, 9 April 2021.

MEAL PLANNING AND COOKING ON A BUDGET

If you have a large freezer and a few gadgets, then you can easily save money and make life simpler at the same time. If you are in poor-quality housing with no freezer and few gadgets, life becomes a bit more complicated, but it's still possible to save. There is, as always, overlap here, so please dive into each section as needed.

Freezers and fridges allow you to store food safely and buy larger quantities if a bargain presents itself. The variety of cooking gadgets listed here, meanwhile, can sometimes save on energy costs – ovens can be quite expensive to run, after all – but not necessarily, so don't just rush out and load up with random bits of equipment. Some of them are expensive and will take a few years to pay for themselves in savings.

Let's start with the gadgets.

Freezers

If you are blessed with a big freezer, you are perfectly situated to take advantage of reduced-price foods – if you see bread and meat or veg reduced to a fraction of their usual price, you can snap them up, hurl them in the freezer and use as needed.

The issue with this is that very often you end up with a surfeit of bread and broccoli and not enough cheese and butter, so it is important to keep a record of what you actually have in the deep freeze, so you are truly able to use the food in a meaningful way. Either keep a pen and notebook tied to the freezer or use a whiteboard marker and use the freezer door to record what lies within.

Meal planning is without doubt the way to go when you have a freezer full of random foods. You can look at what you've got and plan out meals for the week based on what you already have, buying the odd few items to fill in a hole in your ingredients list.

Please remember, though, that frozen food cannot just be refrozen once thawed – it needs cooking first. So, if a large bag of frozen spinach has defrosted, you'll need to turn it into soup before it goes back into the freezer.

The joy of batch cooking, though, is that you cook more labour-intensive meals once but divide them up to be eaten over several days, so a super-organised cook can cook ten enormous dishes and eat them over the course of a month. It may take a little longer to prepare a ragù sauce for ten than it does to prepare one for two (though not by much), but the cost of cooking is considerably reduced.

The energy cost of reheating food matters too, of course, but, obviously, if a meal is cooked and frozen, you can remove it from the freezer at breakfast then just chuck it in the microwave at 6pm.

Freezers work more efficiently when full, as it happens, and, if there is a power cut, a full freezer will stay frozen for far longer than a half-empty one, so, in a pinch, freeze large milk cartons full of water. Keep them upright, of course, as if the power *did* fail, you don't want the freezer full of water – a soggy bread-and-water slurry is a nightmare to dispose of. Equally, keep these appliances free of frost to ensure they're working efficiently – if your freezer keeps frosting up, check the seals carefully, as that may be where the problem is.

Fresh vegetables usually need blanching prior to being frozen: this involves immersing them in boiling water for a few minutes – not for long enough to cook them through but enough to kill any bacteria and enzymes on the surface. We do this to ensure they remain in good condition while frozen and are edible when cooked at a later date. If you live somewhere with allotments, or have friends who grow their own, you may be lucky enough to be given a share of the late-summer surplus. It usually involves tonnes of runner beans and so many courgettes you are sick of the sight of them by the end of August, so a freezer is essential.

Everything you freeze needs sealing properly or you risk the dreaded freezer burn, which is when the outer exposed edges of food become effectively freeze-dried, but not in a good way. It's worth getting a store of very stout plastic bags – you can buy purpose-made ones, but most of us will be able to get hold of suitable bags from general packaging. Clothing often comes in thick plastic, and a heavyweight bag will be washable, so can be reused numerous times. Just use scissors to open at one end and wash the bag out for reuse. A lot of bags now have small holes punched in them for safety (in case a child puts one over their head), which means you need to wrap the contents tightly first, then use the thicker bag to protect the inner, sealed one. When you wash them, just hold the bag filled with water up over the sink to see if it leaks and then sort them accordingly.

A DIY vacuum pack can be effected, meanwhile, by holding on to the top of the bag that you've just filled and immersing the bottom half in water – this drives out the air as it rises to the surface – then tie up the top before removing. To seal them, I use the plastic clips sold at Ikea, but coated wire works just as well and is often to be scrounged from other packaging.

But by all that is holy, LABEL everything! Steak pie with custard is *not* a nice meal, and no matter how much you think you will recognise random frozen objects, it's not worth the risk. In my experience, the easiest and most reliable way is to write a label on a bit of thick card in biro and tuck it into the bag where it will be visible. Stickers come adrift and marker pen smudges more readily than you would think. Make sure you add the date that you froze something too, as frozen food has a freeze life, and it's a matter of months not years. If you freeze fresh food in the original packaging, make a note of the date you removed it from the freezer, as at that point the original use-by-date is irrelevant.

Cold storage

If you are limited on fridge and freezer space, remember that root veg often stores for lengthy periods of time if kept cool, dark and dry. Take things like potatoes and carrots, and most other root vegetables (plus some varieties of squash) and store them in the shed or on a balcony in a secure box. Keep things from touching each other, and ensure ventilation inside the box is good. Check every now and then and remove anything looking slightly past its best. Mice also like veg kept in the shed, unfortunately, so do beware of other creatures feasting off your store.

Slow cookers

Much touted as energy savers, which they are (mostly), but you can't cook everything in a slow cooker, and if it was your only way to cook food, you'd be fed up with soft food pretty quickly. They do, however, mean you can take advantage of foods that take a lot of cooking: dried beans, for example (which, by the way, *must must must* be brought to a rolling boil for ten minutes before dumping into a slow cooker, for safety), and chewy cuts of meat. Sadly, the chewy bits of meat that used to be cheap to buy have become fashionable, so the price has gone up. Don't think you are restricted to stew, though, as you can cook all sorts of stuff. There is a recipe floating around for slow-cooker cheesecake – I absolutely recommend that one. I can't give it here, as it's not mine to share, I'm afraid. I'm sure you can look it up.

Microwaves

It's handy to cook some foods quickly. If you rummage around in charity shops, you will probably find old micro-wave cookery books dating from when they were the latest thing. They really do give you recipes for the most elaborate meals. If you find yourself in digs with only a microwave, I strongly suggest you give these cookbooks a whirl, but have a gander at the ratings plate to see how many watts your model uses, as it really does matter when cooking more complicated stuff.

You can, to be fair, cook an awful lot of things in them, but, like with a slow cooker, they don't brown or crisp food, which is a drawback.

Try to keep the inside as clean as you can – just wipe with a damp cloth after every use.

Air fryers

My air fryer is one of the mini oven types and I use it daily. There is no heat-up time and it browns and crisps food beautifully; the time and temperature are very adjustable and, for small quantities of food, it is excellent. Mine also acts as a dehydrator and so I dried off lots of apple rings to store for winter. To be honest, though, we just ended up eating the dried apple as it came out of the oven . . . The thought was there, but I can't vouch for how long they would have stayed edible, as our greed meant we never got the chance to test it out!

I have no experience at all of the air fryers with a removable 'basket', I'm afraid, but I imagine they are equally useful. The saving with both kinds is because you are heating up a very small space, so there isn't a warm-up time, therefore the food goes in immediately and is cooked faster.

Of course, some food needs spraying with oil prior to cooking or it will become hard and dry rather than crisp, but if you buy an oil spray, read the ingredients and you'll soon realise you can often refill it with normal cooking oil several times over. The other trick is to just brush on the oil – small silicon pastry brushes work well for this.

Multi-purpose 5-in-1 cookers

Some people swear by them, they have numerous models, and use them to cook everything. Mine is in the shed under an inch of dust. My main issue is that they tend to be bulky, and I simply don't have enough room to leave one out all the time. On a daily basis the only function I cannot replicate with other things is the pressure cooking.

The set-up is simple: there is a hotplate hidden in the base, a metal pot then fits inside the unit with a clip-on lid that can be sealed to cook under pressure. Then they have a digital controller that monitors everything and allows fast cooking of everything from cakes to casseroles.

If you get on with them and can afford one, they are excellent things, but they're just not to everybody's liking. Yet the saving here is twofold: firstly, you are heating a small space rather than a large oven, and, secondly, you can cook under pressure, which reduces cooking time considerably.

Pressure cookers

I had a hob-top one many years ago and it was a revelation: things like potatoes cooked in minutes, casseroles and stews were tender in well under an hour and steamed puddings were cooked perfectly. I made neck of lamb stew every night for months – the bony cheap bits of meat along with potatoes, onions and carrots, and plenty of salt and pepper. I think they were largely nudged out of popularity by the microwave, but you can now get electric ones (as well as the 5-in-1 mentioned above) and they are brilliant if you find yourself boiling potatoes every night. If you buy one second-hand, then ensure you replace the rubber gasket and make sure the pressure release valve works properly, as they have a bit of a reputation for exploding.

A hay box

This is a DIY solution and rather old-fashioned, but works a treat – it's literally a box stuffed with hay into which you plunge a pot of hot food. The hay acts as the insulation, you see, retaining the heat, and so the whole thing works like a slow cooker. The modern alternative is an old cool box, or an unwanted polystyrene watercress box scrounged from the greengrocer. You need stuff to pack it out with: old t-shirts are fine, or old polyester wadding, anything at all. Then you prep the dish, say a casserole: brown the meat, add flour, veg, thicken the gravy, and bring to the boil. Put a lid on the casserole and then put into your box.

Surround it with your padding, make sure there is plenty on top, then leave all day. When you come home eight hours later, your meal should be nicely cooked and just need heating up a shade.

Feeding your family on less

Now, I'm not trying to write a cookery book, but, nevertheless, over the coming pages I've included a few quick, cheap and – most importantly – energy-efficient ideas that we use regularly in our household. No one in my family is vegan, however, so I apologise if some of these cannot be veganised easily! Interestingly, if you know how *not* to rely on the meat substitutes (ultra-processed and pricey), it's worth bearing in mind that vegan and vegetarian food often works out far more economical. If you do eat meat, then try to cut it down to two or three meals a week, or just use a tiny shred. For example, I make a chicken BBQ pizza whenever I see precooked chicken sold for sandwich-filling reduced to clear – pizza dough is just strong flour and water with yeast, then I cover it in premade barbecue sauce, plus onions and peppers, etc., with a tiny bit of shredded chicken on top, all covered in cheese. I've never tried substituting chicken with Quorn, say, as I've never had cause to, but it's highly possible it may not be detectable if you do, so feel free to experiment along the same lines.

Buying food

But first things first, as I mentioned earlier in this chapter, if you have ample fridge and freezer space, it pays to make the most of the reduced-price section; if you don't, it can be trickier, but there are a wide range of tinned 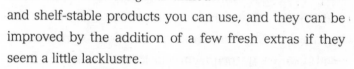 and shelf-stable products you can use, and they can be improved by the addition of a few fresh extras if they seem a little lacklustre.

It's also useful to know that there are several online companies who sell what are known as short-date-coded foods.* This is either food that is still within its best-before date or food that has gone past this date but should still be good to eat. This is all shelf-stable stuff, and they usually give you the date of expiry on the website. For obvious reasons, you are unlikely to get wildly popular stuff, but it's often surprising what these places have, and the stock changes regularly.

---

* Short-date-coded food websites include, among others: approvedfood.co.uk, motatos.co.uk and lowpricefoods.com.

You do have to buy quite a bit, though, so pair up with a friend or two. We once bought lots of branded couscous for about 10p a sachet and, by the time we had got to the last box, were so fed up of it I've never eaten couscous again.

Meal planning

Before any food shopping trip, you need to go through your fridge and freezer to see what you already have in, and what needs using up. Start there and make a rough meal plan for the week. For example, if you have a huge pot of cream and some kale, you could make a kale-and-potato gratin, so perhaps that and sausages tomorrow? The eggs need using, so perhaps a frittata one night? Come up with a meal idea for every night of the week, making sure you account for what you already have, then make a note of what to buy. You are aiming to eliminate food waste by making sure everything gets used.[*]

LISTS

Tomatoes
Peppers
onions
garlic
Apples
Honey
Milk
ham
Bread
Butter

_____

[*]   See p. 133 for more about food waste and the ensuing cost for society as a whole.

Meal planning is there to ensure you don't waste food, and also to make your life easier. You need to be a bit flexible here in case you see something on offer, or something reduced, but you at least have a guide, and you can tidy and wipe out the fridge while you are doing it.

Make notes as you go, and write down what you are planning so you don't forget. You can firm up your meal plan once you have been shopping. Remember to factor in what you are doing on any given day too, as there's no point deciding to do a roast chicken on the night you come home late and exhausted. Something to bear in mind here is that batch cooking, if you can find the time, makes life so much easier: very organised people cook every meal for the week ahead on a Sunday and put it all assembled into the fridge to be reheated on the night. I'm simply not that organised, but I do try to cook and prep double for things that will freeze or keep well. Ragù bolognese can be kept in the fridge, for example, so make extra when you want lasagne and then there will be enough for a quick spaghetti bolognese for later in the week.

Grocery shopping

Strictly speaking, doing a big weekly shop is the best way to save: you make a meal plan and stick to it. That does presuppose you have storage for a week's worth of food, of course, and not everyone does. If not, try to stick to your meal plan for food you already have, and make sure you only buy what is needed with any top-up shop.

A big saver is to knock the booze on the head. It's well known that many of us started drinking quite a lot during lockdown and never stopped, and I know a lot of families who drink a bottle of wine a night. Kicking the drinking will be a huge bonus for your health as well as your pocket. It's easy to drift slowly into drinking every day, but if you must drink, keep it for social events rather than a wet Tuesday.

If you plan to go in person to shop, eat before you leave the house, as going shopping for food while slightly peckish adds at least £50 to the end bill. And make a list not just for the meal plan but for everything else: walk around the house and check supplies. Don't just buy on autopilot or you end up with five bottles of conditioner and no shampoo.

Look carefully at special offers – do you really need them? Are you just being coerced into buying more than you will need? Are they saving you money? That's not always a given, to be honest.

I have mentioned this before, but always look carefully at *all* the shelves in a section, as the ones at eye level may not be the best value. It is also usually cheaper to buy vegetables and fruit loose rather than prepacked, and it's always preferable to buy what you will use rather than get an economy pack of fruit then throw most of it away untouched.

If you are shopping online, it is easier to avoid temptation (but not impossible) and, of course, you can just get up and check the cupboards for ketchup before you buy yet another bottle. You still need a list, though, and a meal plan. Look for the cheap delivery slots – one supermarket near us will deliver at 11pm for £1.50. I'm always asleep by then, but if you are a night owl then it's well worth getting those later slots, and sometimes the driver will ring to deliver much earlier as they might be ahead of schedule and so can finish their shift early once you have taken your delivery.

Wartime lessons and cooperation

The other source of excellent budget- and energy-friendly ideas are the wartime leaflets from the Ministry of Food – you may not be aware that rationing was in full force until the 50s in Britain, and the nation's health actually improved because of it. Everyone received a ration designed to keep them in good health, but as that was an equal share of the limited amount available, for some people it was the first time they had had access to a relatively balanced diet, one that was also low in both meat and, most importantly, sugar.

Similarly egalitarian, a while back my mother set up a wholefood co-operative group and it worked well for many years. I seem to remember that there was a lot of working out who got what, as not everyone wanted a 25kg sack of flour, so you would team up with four others, say, and divvy out the flour. The idea was that you found a group of like-minded people and then bulk-bought food at wholesale prices, which then saves everyone money. It's unlikely to be cheaper than somewhere like Tesco or Asda (though it can depend what it is), but they all lived remotely and, for them, it meant they had access to stuff like grains, flour and pulses for sensible prices – much less packaging too, which is a big plus environmentally. This approach may well prove to be practical for you too if you live remotely and/or tend to cook from scratch a lot.

Jam today, jam tomorrow

But the thing you may remember from books set a few generations ago, both during and between the wars, is jam – they made lots of the stuff. Jam is a good way of preserving fruit, especially wild fruit. You boil it with sugar – roughly 50/50 – and pectin too, if it needs it (some fruits don't, and you can get special 'jam sugar' that has pectin added), until it reaches setting point and it coagulates. You then pour it into sterile jars, pop a small wax paper disc over the surface and then a cellophane cover, which is fixed with a rubber band over the jar. Stored well, it keeps for years. Jams, pickles and chutneys are all ways to preserve fruit and veg without needing a fridge or freezer.

The big 'but' in this scenario is that there is only so much chutney, say, one family can or will eat in a year – you can give some away, and in small jars it does make a nice present, but make sure you don't get carried away.

You can also use Kilner jars to preserve stuff. In America they do what is referred to as 'canning', and the kit to process food is easily accessible and afficionados can put virtually everything edible into the 'cans', which are usually glass jars. I know several people who spend all summer canning up food to feed themselves during the winter. This is especially useful in remote areas where extreme weather affects power, and the community is cut off for extended periods of time. It also means they can buy food when it is cheap and eat it later in the year when prices are high. Or there are some lucky souls who manage to grow everything. This approach is not so common in the UK, however; what is more usual is the process of storing more acidic fruit and veg in jars. You can do this with reused jam jars – if you look, there is a line of rubber stuck to the metal, and as long as the lid is straight and the rubber intact, you should be able to reuse the jar. The Kilner jars can be quite expensive but are reusable, so if you think you will preserve fruit in the future, it may be worth investing, but if you only use the jar once, it simply isn't worth buying. I frequently preserve apples and blackberries in jars for use in pies and crumbles – it's not difficult and saves freezer space. Rather than me explain how to do it here, though, I suggest you find a good book or check online. I have never done canning, so I'm not going to comment in case I get it wrong, and you accidentally get botulism!

Community food-sharing groups

Check to see if there are any community food-sharing groups near you or a community pantry – these are also good for those who don't have much space to store foods. Our local one has several people who use the Too Good To Go app: they buy the very short-dated food and share it out among themselves. If there isn't such a group, maybe consider setting one up and make sure it's easily accessible to those who really need it?

If you are struggling, then please do find out how to get food from a food bank: the method varies, as some places require a voucher and limit you to the number of times you can claim, while others allow you to just turn up. There is no shame in needing help – it's important you understand that. Accept help when you need it and give help when you can.

If you are lucky enough to be able to afford food, then please donate to food banks regularly, either with money or by giving what they ask for.

Things to think about when donating to food banks

Living on economy tins is miserable

Women and girls need sanitary products

Nice shampoo and conditioner cheer people up

Cleaning products and laundry products are also needed

Not everyone has access to a cooker

People have pets (and should have pets, as they improve mental health)

That last point above has historical connotations: at one point, if you had 'the welfare' come round and means test you for what was then called parish aid, the dog had to be taken out for a long walk, as it was felt that if you had surplus to feed a pet, you had enough money to survive without help. They also checked for 'signs of comfort' – to get help you had to be pretty much destitute; it's one reason some older people are so frightened to get help. I recently did a little digging and discovered that work-houses continued in some form or another well into the 40s and, in fact, some were transferred to the control of hospitals and run as 'reception centres for wayfarers' (casual wards for vagrants, i.e. rough sleepers) until the

1960s! Sadly, it seems our supposedly modern welfare system is turning back the clock to those times . . . how soon we forget.

What works for you

Cooking from scratch is not *always* cheaper – the cost of the actual cooking and all the little added extras mount up. You may only be using a teaspoon of spice (cost 3p), but you had to buy the whole damn tin (cost £1.69) and may well not use it all before it goes stale. It also takes time, and very often you don't have time. During lockdown I cooked and baked daily. Pastries, cakes, casseroles and lots of interesting veg; now I am back at work, it's all I can manage to snarf a sandwich.

Do whatever works for your lifestyle and refuse to feel guilty about it no matter what anyone else says. Do be aware, though, that with packaged food you pay for the cost of processing, but, to be fair, that cost can be quite low, as mechanisation and economies of scale mean a tonne of carrots can be processed almost as quickly as you process a few kilos. That said, you may also find you pay by not buying the quality you might get from making it yourself. Remember to be savvy with your choices.

The food industry uses what they refer to as 'value-added' products to increase profitability, you see – a value-added product is a basic foodstuff enhanced by some extra process or ingredient. Some of these additions do indeed add value, i.e. those washed potatoes and carrots save time, while granola is easier to grab from a packet and can be costly to make at home. Other things may not be such good value. Look at the amount of chicken in a ready-made pie: you certainly save time and effort not making the pie, and it's not likely to be much more expensive than a home-made pie, maybe even cheaper, but there is a lot less chicken in it than one you make at home, and you may not be getting as many nutrients for the amount of calories.

You also need to try to keep an eye on things like fat and salt, as quite a lot of preprepared dishes are high in both, as they scrimp on the basic ingredients to turn a profit then add extra fat and salt so that it still tastes nice. If you can add in a good helping of veg to anything shop-bought, however, you'll help bulk it out and make your gut happy while keeping your intake of both salt and fat to a minimum.

If you are cooking at home, then by all means take a leaf out of the food producers' book and use padding, but try to keep your padding nutritious. Minced beef, for example, can be stretched to breaking point with grated carrots, porridge oats, a stock cube, and vegetables in general. Lentils work well if you like them (my son wishes it to be known that lentils are nasty, just in case I get any ideas about trying to sneak any into the food he eats), and in many dishes it's worth looking up a vegetarian version, as even if you aren't veggie, you can use the suggestions to pad out the meat. I found that chestnuts, button mushrooms and small onions can stretch a beef casserole out a very long way indeed. My own personal high point of padding out a meal was, after buying a high-end vegetarian lasagne that used a lentil and mushroom ragù as its base, I made my own version of the ragù, but with a little mince added to appease the resolute meat eaters.

Cheap meals

An economical and easy option if you want to take some pressure off your budget is to make more soup – it's infinitely variable, can be incredibly cheap, and uses only one pan. Just as importantly, it's a great way to get lots of veg into both yourself and the children, and it's amazing how many leftovers can be hurled into it. I suggest you blend baked beans, though, as while a delicious addition to many soups, they do stand out rather.

Soup is pretty much liquidised food. Plenty of recipes are to be found online, but don't feel obliged to be precise. I've kept my family alive on vegetable soup for quite extended periods – potatoes, carrots, onion and anything else cheap, cooked in water with a stock cube, blended, and then with either some cream or some milk added to enrich it. You can beat an egg into it too (but keep below boiling after that, as scrambled egg in soup can be weird).

I've also lived on pretty much nothing but baked beans on wholemeal toast for months. It's quite a balanced meal if you add a piece of fruit for pudding. Boring, admittedly, but cheap and nutritious.

Making things stretch

My mother's point about adding carrots to everything (as mentioned in the introduction) is sound, but throughout my childhood it was generally spring greens (i.e. young cabbage) with everything. Most weeks, when I was growing up, a small joint of meat was bought and roasted on Sunday, with leftovers served in various incarnations all week until Friday (which was always fish), and Saturday was an egg dish. The meat was stretched out with potatoes and mountains of greens. My grandmother wasn't a good cook, unfortunately, and so her food wasn't particularly enjoyable. Pudding was either blancmange, stewed fruit, or tinned rice pudding. I hated all of it due to the texture, but have to admit it was perfectly healthy if monotonous.

Which leads me to the subject of variety. Prior to the days of airfreighted food, much of our fruit and veg in this country was seasonal, which arguably led to greater variety in some ways, as we had to eat with the seasons rather than buying the same thing every week (though what was referred to as the 'hungry gap' in early spring, when little to no fresh produce was in season, could be tricky). Strawberries were prized, as they could only be bought during the summer months and were associated with warm sunny days. Apples came into season in the late summer, and by Christmas only certain varieties that stored well were available in the shops, so a Cox's Orange Pippin was often found in the toe of the Christmas stocking. Despite the onslaught of imported veg nowadays, we must remember that we do still have wonderful seasonal veg in the UK, and due to the low transport costs, it provides excellent value, but the seasonal nature of it means you don't get as bored as you might with yet another tasteless imported tomato. And it's often better for you as well as being tastier too.

As a rule, meat (and meat substitutes) tends to be the most expensive item on a plate, so cut that back to a very small sliver and fill the plate up with cheap veg instead, ensuring you use a variety rather than just greens. If you have only a microwave, then the sachets of mixed veg work out economically. Obviously not as cheap as cooked individually, but factor in time and energy and it's not unreasonable – there is no waste either.

The starchy part of a meal is often the most filling, be it rice, potatoes or something like lentils, but do try to avoid eating carbs to the exclusion of other veg. While cheap and filling, you really will feel better with a decent input of other veg, be it fresh, frozen or tinned. Living frugally often requires you to expend energy in lieu of cash and a good diet can really help with that slightly sluggish feeling you can get after eating too many starchy meals. If you are not eating animal products, you may well wonder about protein. It was once considered that pairing a pulse (containing lysine) with a grain (containing methionine) was necessary to provide all essential amino acids, but as we now know the liver can store these, it is not necessary to always eat them in the same meal anymore. Many cultures have wonderful dishes pairing the two that are well worth exploring, however, and very often looking at traditional one-pan meals is a great way to find nutritionally balanced and extremely tasty food.

While I'm on the subject, if you decide to go vegan, or are vegan already, you may or may not be aware that there are a few nutrients you need to be careful about. Vitamins B12 and D can be lacking – vitamin D means getting outside and letting your skin absorb the sun, but in winter a supplement might be a good idea. Iodine may be a little low too, so make sure you use iodised salt and eat seaweed, soy milk and prunes. Realistically, if you are either vegetarian or vegan, it is worth taking a good vitamin and mineral supplement just to make absolutely sure you are getting your full complement of nutrients.

Food waste

In the immediate post-war years, food was still rationed strictly, and nothing was wasted – the smallest morsel of food was reused without question, with only unusable leftovers going to either the pig or to the chickens. Food waste today is a massive problem; we have become accustomed to cheap food and think nothing of discarding things we cannot eat before they go bad. To help combat this, many retailers are now removing best before dates from food and once again are relying on consumers to use their eyes and nose to determine if food is edible rather than throwing away perfectly good produce. There are people out there who live on discarded food taken from waste bins behind supermarkets, taking mountains of perfectly good edible produce which has been discarded for being unsaleable. We pay for that: the cost of that waste is factored into the price we pay at the till. If, as a society, we commit to reducing this waste, our food costs may reduce too, not just because you aren't chucking out £5 worth of food you forgot to eat, but because retailers wouldn't need to add in the disposal costs to their budget, but it's UK households who are the biggest problem.

According to website Wastemanaged.co.uk, the UK produces around 9.5 million tonnes of food waste per year, of which 70% comes from households. Of this, 6.4 million tonnes could have been eaten: that works out at between £250 to £400 per household.

I have a glorious little book published by the Berkshire Women's Institute in 1944 and a lot of the recipes involve using leftovers. A rather useful one is for savoury pancakes, and I often wonder if this is the origin of the Findus crispy pancake so popular during the 70s . . .

Stuffed pancakes

Make pancakes [thin, crêpe-style ones] in the usual way but they may be fried in dripping. Have ready any scraps of meat, vegetables etc. A small piece of bacon minced is a good addition to anything savoury. Heat the scraps carefully in a saucepan, adding a little gravy if necessary, fold the heated filling in the pancakes and serve hot with chipped potatoes.

I have tried this recipe myself and it's really rather nice, but I put the rolled pancakes into the frying pan and heated them so the pancake was slightly crispy on the underside. It also works very well with leftover macaroni cheese or cauliflower cheese stuffed inside.

Another idea is something the Berkshire WI call 'scrap roast', which involves mashing finely chopped onions and a few herbs with cooked lentils and stale breadcrumbs, then mixing in finely chopped leftover roast meat, seasoning well and pressing the mixture into a baking dish and baking it in a medium oven until browned. I've actually done something similar with mushrooms too – sauté a large pack of mushrooms, sliced, with a chopped sweet pepper (or two, but then have one green and one red) plus an onion, finely sliced. Chop the cooked mixture finely (or zap in a food processor) then mix with bread-crumbs and grated cheese. Bake until brown and voilà!

Cooking bacon

Just so my mother's point about bacon isn't wasted (see the introduction for her distillation of being frugal), 'cooking bacon' is just offcuts and can actually be quite large chunks of salty bacon. It's tasty and cheap, but useless for a fry-up. So make a clanger instead. Tradi-tionally this is rolled up like a swiss roll and steamed (in a floured clean tea towel), but I do it in a bowl so I can use my slow cooker. What you need is a heat-resistant bowl or casserole that fits in your slow cooker with room for water around it: you don't need a lid, as tinfoil will do.

Clanger

250g self-raising flour to 125g suet
(basically, it's half fat to flour in the proportion
you need for the dish you are using)

Mix together with cold water to make a soft dough. Line your bowl with the suet crust, leaving enough for a lid and a mid-point layer of suet pastry.

Chop cooking bacon into small bits, likewise an onion (use a white one as red onion goes a funny colour) and, if you enjoy it, mix in half a packet of reconstituted sage-and-onion stuffing (the stuffing is cheaper than the bacon, so as well as adding flavour, it bulks out the bacon). Make sure the stuffing is quite moist, and don't drain the bacon, as you need liquid to ensure the middle is nice and tender. Spoon half the bacon mix into the lined basin, add your middle floor of pastry and tip the rest on top. Put on the pastry lid and seal by pinching closed with wet fingers. Top with a circle of greaseproof or a butter wrapper, then cover the whole lot in tinfoil. Make sure there is headroom for the clanger to rise as it cooks, and fold over the foil carefully round the edges of the bowl so the water doesn't seep inside. Put it in to your slow cooker, fill up to the edge of the pudding bowl with boiling water and leave on low setting all day.

Serve with peas, and gravy if you like it. It's a very filling meal for a cold night.

Always keep in mind that all the traditional ways of stretching food involved variations on basic tricks that are easily replicated. Yorkshire puddings were often served before the main course, for example, and those who ate the most Yorkshires traditionally got the most meat, but, of course, after eating a mountain of Yorkshire puds, the largest appetite was dulled.

A lot of traditional British food is calorie rich: suet puddings both savoury and sweet, pies and dumplings all feature. Made well, they are light and delicious and fuel a body through the winter cold.

When it came to dessert, rice pudding, suet pudding and fruit pies have all long been sterling ways to fill a gap. If you cannot get free windfall apples in autumn to dry or freeze for later, then make sure you buy the right kind of apple for your purpose. Cooking apples fluff up when cooked into a light puree, while eating apples remain in shape and can be a little leathery; some puddings need this but make sure to check. Tarte Tatin, for example, requires eating apples, but apple crumble works far better with a cooking variety. A baked apple (core a large cooking apple, stuff with a mixture of butter, sugar and some raisins, wrap in foil then bake for around an hour) is a dish not often seen today and is totally delicious, but, to be economical, you need to bake a lot at once or tuck a few in the oven while other things are baking. And to stretch it a little further, wrap the cored and stuffed apple in suet pastry and bake until golden, then serve with custard or cream. Yum!

When my children were at the human dustbin stage, I made a lot of cake. My standard recipe comes from *The Radiation Cookery Book*, published in 1921, and is incredibly flexible. You can add more eggs or fat if you have them, add dried fruit, or chocolate chips, cherries or anything you have that you need to use up. Slice some apples or a pear into the baking tin before pouring in the cake batter and it makes a great pudding with custard.

Cake

250g flour

Generous teaspoon baking powder

50g fat (honestly, butter, lard – it doesn't matter)

75g sugar (or less – brown or white is fine)

1 egg

Milk to mix

It's a rubbed-in cake, so rub fat into flour (or whiz together in the food processor) then add everything else so it is a soft dropping consistency. Bake for just over an hour in a greased tin at Gas Mark 3 (165C or 150C in a fan oven).

With such a low amount of fat, this cake doesn't keep terribly well – about a week in a tightly lidded tin, but that's rarely a problem. You can add in more fat and sugar to make it keep longer, or remove some of the flour and replace it with cocoa powder, or put dollops into paper cases to make rock cakes. If you cannot get, or afford, an egg, replace the egg with a little vinegar and water. Or replace the milk with yoghurt that needs using up.

Ways with bread

Stale bread is incredibly useful stuff – you can turn it into crumbs for breading food to be fried, use it to make stuffing, and add it to mince for a meatloaf or to make a nut roast. I often make a cheese pudding for myself if I have the heel of a loaf and some rather noisy cheese – I mix a cup of breadcrumbs with a generous helping of assorted cheese, salt, pepper and a spoonful of mustard. Beat two or three eggs well together, add a dash of Worcestershire sauce and then beat this mixture into the breadcrumbs. Put in a baking dish and bake at 190C until well risen and golden brown. Serve with salad.

Bread pudding, or bread-and-butter pudding, are both delicious ways to fill an empty hole, and I've noticed queen of puddings seems to have gone out of vogue so, with no further ado:

Queen of Puddings

(recipe taken from *From Hand To Mouth*, Berkshire Federation of Women's Institutes, 1944)

475ml milk
90g white breadcrumbs
60g butter
3 eggs
Sugar to taste

Bring milk to boil then stir in the butter and the sugar and the crumbs and leave to cool. Meanwhile separate the eggs and, once cool, beat the egg yolks well into the mixture and pour into a dish. Bake in a moderate oven [I use about 160C fan] until just set. Remove from oven and set to one side. Beat egg whites stiffly and then beat in a tablespoon of sugar until the meringue is still and glossy. Gently spread the jam on top of the pudding and spread the meringue on top, put into oven until the top is nicely browned.

[My preference is for either blackberry jam or raspberry, but use what you have and like.]

Growing your own

Many people grow their own veg, and for a skilled and keen gardener, it is very much possible to grow the majority of your food. It takes work, though; you can't just throw a few seeds in the ground and come back to a full harvest. I've seen some truly inspirational set-ups in tiny urban gardens, and in Britain we are lucky to have allotments. These are small plots of land rented from the council. My friend in County Durham has a massive allotment with a shed, electricity and chickens. In my own town the allotments are small strips upon which you are allowed a sentry-box shed, with no power and a no-livestock rule, so be aware that there is considerable variation in how allotments are set up.

If you are keen and can spare the time and energy to try to grow veg but have no garden, then ask your local council about an allotment. But if you have a balcony or a tiny patch of ground, it is worth investigating vertical gardens – every square inch of space, including walls, is devoted to growing all sorts of veg, and the results are truly impressive.

However, don't invest too much money until you are sure you can actually grow the veg you plan to eat. The trick is to grow a wide variety, so you aren't overwhelmed with carrots and cabbage. Don't plant too many potatoes either, unless you eat pounds of them. Remember all fruit and veg must be stored before eating, so while growing 45 kilos of green beans is quite exciting, you then have to store them. Likewise, courgettes, which often result in gluts.

I once grew ten spaghetti squash plants; I had no idea they got so big, and they produced about ten squash per plant. I was giving them to people so often that they started to cross the road to avoid me in case I gave them another squash. In the end, I left them to rot. Then, the following year, I had to uproot numerous healthy squash seedlings. The bloody things were still appearing several years later. Horseradish spreads, as do Jerusalem arti-chokes, so plant in large pots. Likewise mint . . . it's so robust it counts as a weed.

I suggest you read a few comprehensive guides and get to know a few good growers, as most gardeners will chew your ear off about growing onions, if that's their thing, or making great compost. You can learn a lot, and if you are on an allotment, you can learn how other people solved problems you may well face yourself. Certain soils and conditions bring challenges peculiar to your location, and you may find some plants won't thrive where you are. Sharing seeds and excess seedlings is a great way to get plants which will 'do well' locally, however.

Things to note: compost – this is gold. A good compost heap does wonders for any soil, so learn the art of compost. It means nothing plant-based is wasted, but food waste needs a bokashi system and they can work out as expensive, so wait to see if you are going to be a constant gardener before you buy one. Likewise, if you ever see bags of horse manure offered for free, grab them, but they must rot before being put on your soil or they risk burning crops.

You also absolutely need wellies . . . and gloves.

Look after your tools. A clean sharp spade makes trenching fairly easy (I was tempted to say effortless, but your back will ache no matter what). Don't leave them outside in the rain to rust; get into the habit of wiping them clean with an oily rag every time you finish. It's worth buying a really good pair of secateurs, then painting the handles bright orange. If you can tie them to a wrist loop or to your belt, I advise it, as they get lost and only turn up once you have bought a second ruinously expensive pair.

I have a similar problem with trowels – I've got four at present . . .

A small greenhouse is incredibly useful, as you can get seeds off to an early start, and if it's a poor summer, some of the less robust crops, such as aubergines and peppers, can be moved in to finish ripening (only if they are in pots, though), but as with everything, don't fork out a large amount until you are sure you will get your money's worth. They do crop up occasionally on our local buy-and-sell groups, or you can fashion one from timber and bubble wrap, but be aware that it won't withstand heavy wind.

Do not leave garden waste lurking, as it can spread disease, but nice little twiggy heaps encourage insect life, and hedgehogs adore them because that insect life is their dinner. Pesticides: please try not to. Slug pellets kill shrews, hedgehogs and birds if they eat contaminated slugs. Use barriers to protect tender plants, and encouraging wildlife will give you natural protection too. There are also nematodes to kill slugs – microscopic pests that you water into the soil. Likewise other pests: always use the least harmful way of dealing with them, remembering that you eat the plants, so encourage a healthy ecosystem, with as much diversity as possible.

Try not to grow jumbo veg unless you are competing for the largest onion in a local show – young vegetables are sweet and tender; old ones are frequently hard and tasteless. Make sure to grow things that are enjoyable – the raspberry patch is what I miss most about my old garden. We only ever ate them off the canes, the dog getting the lowest fruit and my son the stuff at the back. A fig tree takes years to mature, but on a south-facing wall you can often have figs within a few years, and a sun-warmed fig, fresh from the tree, is a glorious thing. I live in the South of England and have yet to find a grape vine that produces sweet grapes, but I know they make good wine. I suspect we simply don't have the weather for the dessert varieties.

I know many will disagree, but I reckon that if you must choose what to grow, it makes sense to grow the expensive luxury stuff. Potatoes and carrots are at the cheap end of the market, and while homegrown can have better flavour, it's growing your own asparagus that saves the money. Rhubarb is fantastic if you like it and comes back every year with very little work. Having said that, a vegan friend of mine grows most of her own beans. Every year she puts up five or six plants each of various types of beans, leaving them to fully ripen and dry on the plant, then she dries them further and stores them in jars.

In spring she just takes five beans out of each jar and plants them – over the course of many years she has evolved really hardy and productive bean plants, and as they are trained upwards on a trellis, they take up very little space.

The other benefit of growing your own is the satisfaction. Instead of using your spare time spending your hard-earned cash on crap you really don't need, you are outside in the fresh air (and pelting rain, hail and howling gale) producing your food for the oncoming year. It is fulfilling, and strangely addictive. I can honestly say that I have sat on an old chair, in a quagmire of mud after digging nettles, and been as content as I have ever been . . .

SHOPPING SMARTER

Buy, buy, buy?

At the risk of repeating myself for the umpteenth time: you have been trained to consume. So, the very first priority is to learn how to recognise that training kicking in, and then combat it. I've mentioned in earlier chapters how much companies spend tracking the behaviour of shoppers: what colours make you feel 'safe', what smells make you buy things and so on. If you become alert to these tricks, they do lose their power somewhat. Not completely, of course, but enough.

Some further basic things to remember: want and need are *very* different categories, and sometimes what you want is not good for you. Equally, only satisfying needs can make you miserable, so don't deny yourself everything that is nice, as in the end it is counter-productive. Sometimes you need frippery, but make sure that frippery is satisfying enough to warrant the outlay. Leave credit cards at home. In fact, it's wisest to leave all your cards at home and take cash instead, though our increasingly cashless society can make this tricky. Plus, some expenditure benefits from having the ability to charge back through the card provider (i.e. cashback, vouchers, loyalty points and buyer protections). But for in-person shopping, you should be fine as long as you keep the receipt. Keep a stout envelope somewhere and regularly empty out your wallet or purse and put all your receipts in it. Then, once a month, go through them and discard all the ones you definitely won't need at a later date.

Simply put, advertising works. It works *incredibly* well. So try to cut yourself off from it as much as is possible. I often tell the tale of how, many years ago, I had not watched television for about 6–9 months – not deliberately, but it just happened that way. I live in a small country town with no hoardings and really couldn't afford magazines, so hadn't seen any advertisements for ages. I went to see a film with a friend – *Sex and the City* – and enjoyed it enormously for all the froth and glamour. Before we drove home, however, my friend and I called into Boots to grab something small and, as I walked past the cosmetics counter, a little voice inside my head told me how much better my life would be if I bought some of the pretty jars. It was so alien a thought by that point that I noticed it; I really noticed it – like a malignant little imp in my head urging me to buy things. It took me a while, but then I realised it was the film, and also the lovely enticing display in the pharmacy. Once I spotted what was happening, I could, of course, walk away, but since that revelation I've consciously avoided TV and magazines as much as possible. I don't like being made to feel badly about myself simply to manipulate me into buying things.

How to shop smarter

Now, I often suggest buying second-hand. I've done it for so long I doubt I will ever be sold on buying new again. Second-hand has the extra dimension of the hunt too, which I enjoy – you see so much that doesn't fit, doesn't suit you or that you plain dislike that the discovery of the perfect item is exhilarating. You need to be discerning, of course, as there's no point buying the perfect pair of trousers if they are too tight, even if they are only 50p, but a skilled seamstress can work wonders on things that are maybe a little too large, so it helps to know what can and cannot be adjusted and adapted.

However, if you need something and haven't been able to buy it second-hand, then you may need to hit the shops. Make a list, and make sure it's a detailed list. Decide what you want – a knee-length dress suitable for the Christmas party and your aunt May's funeral, perhaps? Black, navy or charcoal grey? Do you need shoes? Check first to see what you have. Will you need tights? Now set a budget: an amount you cannot afford to go over. Leave your cards at home and take the cash. Then go only to shops that sell women's clothing, and go straight to the dress section. Do not pause in the cosmetics section, and avoid the towel display! You want a dress, not a poinsettia. Look at dresses, try a few on. Do they all fit? Are they comfortable (that's two back on display)? Will they need dry-cleaning or fiddly ironing (another two bite the dust)? Then take a picture of the candidates. Go and try a few more else-where, then sit down somewhere quiet and look through the pictures. Once you are totally sure that is the outfit you want, go back and buy it. Avoid the food hall coming back . . . (my tip is to take sandwiches if you are likely to get peckish).

Despite sounding rather draconian, your life is made far easier when you only buy things that are exactly what you want and need. It's alarmingly easy to get distracted into buying something not quite right when you have the weight of billions of pounds spent on marketing influencing you to spend money. Don't settle!

Clothing

We all need to wear clothes. Even in warmer climes, complete nudity is rarely accepted. It's an expense we simply cannot avoid.

Going back in time to preindustrial communities, clothing was a huge expense. Weaving and producing cloth took both time and skill, and clothing was valuable, which ensured it was mended and repaired until not a single scrap of cloth could be reused. The very poor usually only had the one set of clothes and those had been handed on so many times they were close to rags.

In our modern age, the growth of fast fashion has become a scourge. The temptation to buy the cheapest garment possible, wearing it twice and then discarding it has created mountains of waste in hidden places; a vast number of things donated to charity end up blowing in the wind of a far-flung landfill site.

The other night I was idly browsing online and noticed the prevalence of a particularly odd phrase: 'Dress for the Life You Want, Not the Life You Have'. It's rather stupid, don't you think? On the surface it's just a quirky way of saying that nice clothes can cheer you up, and that's true, of course. But just think about what would happen if you did just that? I know – I tried it. I ended up with lots of pairs of amazing high-heeled boots, several stunning dresses and two sheer silk caftans. I still have the caftans, but I also have a dog with fur like Velcro and claws that would shred the silk in seconds. I was misguidedly spending money on things I would simply never wear, because I'm a middle-aged rural cleaner with sore feet and a bike. When on earth would I wear those lovely boots? How can I ride a bike in a dress? Those purchases didn't make the life I wanted happen, because that would have required a major overhaul: moving, abdicating responsibility for my children and having surgery on my feet. All I'd done was waste money on clothes I never wore. Which was the underlying point all along: it's no coincidence that every blog where I saw that particular phrase had a shop attached to it . . .

Ignoring the ecological disaster that budget clothing has created for one moment, there is equally an economic one associated with that aspect of the industry. Many people find they cannot afford good quality clothing, so they buy the cheap imports instead, which then only survive a few washes, after which they must purchase more. The horrible irony of this conundrum is that, as we've discussed in previous chapters, it's particularly expensive being poor.*

But learning to mend your clothes helps. Anyone bothering to darn their socks, however, is relatively unusual today, as most people find it easier just to throw worn socks away and buy new. Admittedly, darning a hand-knitted woollen sock makes more sense than repairing a cheap cotton sports sock, but the process of darning isn't terribly difficult and, even if you only repair each sock once, you will reduce your hosiery bill significantly. And if your big toe tends to poke through within a few wears, you may only need to stitch up the hole rather

---

* Google 'Terry Pratchett and the Sam Vimes "Boots" theory of socio-economic unfairness' to see this concept explained beautifully.

than darn it (but investigate cutting your toenails more frequently too).

Mending holes in pockets and sewing on buttons, meanwhile, are easy jobs requiring very little skill, and once you have got the hang of doing that sort of thing, it is just a small step to repairing small splits in seams and other similar tasks. It's well worth looking online for inspiration from the 'visible mending' trend: it involves turning repairs into small, embroidered patches, for example, instead of trying to make the repair invisible, and is well worth considering as an approach if it seems a repair won't be invisible no matter what you do or how skilled you are. In the 1970s it was very fashionable for bell-bottomed jeans to be covered in patches and repairs; a trend perhaps driven by the cost of a new pair of Levi's. I have a small darning loom and I use it a lot. I can produce a perfectly neat and tight darn on almost anything, and rather than make them invisible, I often use thread that's a bright contrast to the garment, just to show off my skill.*

---

* Invisible mending often needs you to get a perfect match in thread to the garment being repaired. However, if you can turn it inside out, you can often take threads from the seam allowances inside, which makes life easier. Though some manufacturers provide extra thread and buttons at purchase, so it helps to keep hold of them in a handy tin somewhere with all your other mending kit.

For those of you with a dash of crafting creativity and a sewing machine, however, a whole world of alteration opens. Just be sure to start with simple projects: take your time and you will find that your skill and confidence grows quickly. Even cheap fast fashion can be tweaked to last longer (resewing flimsy seams and making sure buttons are firmly attached prior to wear can extend the life of a shirt by months) and fit better, but making clothes at home is not the cheap option it once was, as fabric is increasingly expensive. However, it can be a deeply satisfying exercise. I know several very clever people who buy garments made from good fabric at a charity shop then completely recut and remake the entire item, and it's quite startling the results they achieve: one-off pieces of clothing that fit perfectly and ooze style.

Yet it's buying second-hand where you can really reap dividends, as you can often buy a better-quality pair of jeans, for example, second-hand than you can new, as you're not paying the premium for 'newness'. Virtually everything I wear is second-hand, and I make it a point to buy the very best quality that I possibly can, then wash my clothes carefully and mend them as they show wear and tear over time. Again, if you are handy with a sewing machine, you can alter things to fit perfectly, and for some garments it may even pay to get a tailor to modify things for you. One friend bought a very expensive mother-of-the-bride outfit from eBay, which was rather dated, with a thigh-length jacket. With the help of a good tailor, she had the jacket shortened to waist length and the excess material fashioned into a fascinator. She looked perfect, saved a small fortune, gave work to a small business and then sold the outfit afterwards for not a lot less than she paid for it.

Children

Baby clothes are grown out of in weeks rather than months, and you genuinely don't need mountains of new clothes for a baby. Very often parents are given oodles of attractive outfits but the child grows so fast that half of them aren't worn. Car boot sales used to be groaning with brand new, unworn baby clothes, prams and pushchairs in immaculate condition, cot toys and preschool toys, though much of this has drifted onto the Facebook buy-and-sell groups now, as it's far easier than getting up at 7am to stand watching a stranger trying to buy an expensive, immaculate baby buggy for 10p. Apps such as Vinted, eBay and Preloved make buying second-hand easy too. Babies don't care if their clothes are slightly marked with tomato sauce, and toys can be washed and dried for hygiene, which allows you to put the money you have saved towards something else.

Children grow fast, so buying new always seems pointless, as either they outgrow garments before they are even remotely worn out or ruin them within days (parents of primary-school-age children know well the pain of uniforms with holes and ingrained mud within the first week of term). Due to this, buying 'preloved' clothes for children has become incredibly popular, and it's far easier to buy clothes for a toddler while sat on your sofa than wrestling them and the buggy around the shops. Sit in comfort while they sleep, with a mug of tea and some biscuits to hand, and browse for bargains.

I often get asked about stain removal from play clothes, and, yes, often you can get things properly clean, but, for everyone's sanity, it's easier to have several sets of 'rough' clothes, which can be covered in paint and mud without anyone getting too uptight. Clean doesn't always mean spotless, and children certainly don't need to be spotless all the time. I'm sure many of you remember being shouted at for ruining good clothes. Both Tom Kitten and Peter Rabbit got into frightful trouble, I seem to recall, but I always thought it should have been a cautionary tale, not for children but for parents. Had Peter and Tom been dressed in suitable play clothes, they might have escaped with their outfits intact.

As a child, all my clothes were handmade, crafted from reused fabric by my grandmother, with deep hems and massive seam allowances, so they could be let out as I grew. I'm afraid I always looked a little strange and old-fashioned, and consequently was beaten up weekly. I yearned for a flimsy nylon dress bought new from Tammy, the fashionable shop back then – but, alas, our income did not stretch to such frightful expense. Instead, I had to travel in a handmade tweed 'costume', complete with matching gloves and a hat, in 1973. I could have died of embarrassment.*

My siblings lived in cast-offs – hard-wearing items would do the rounds of local children for many years (I remember an old party frock of mine turned up in a school photo on a totally unknown child about ten years after I outgrew it), and while mostly they didn't mind, a few new items were always appreciated. Luckily, all the other

---

* It would probably be quite fashionable now – check out the 'sad beige children' parody accounts on social media, which poke gentle fun at the fashion for dressing children like Victorian urchins.

children in our circle were in the same boat, so they weren't quite as traumatised as I sometimes felt by odd clothes, sometimes long past their best.

While second-hand is a brilliant way to save money, do be critical and make sure the items don't look odd, or shabby. And it can be wise to try to avoid having highly distinctive garments too often, as to be sure their classmates, or older sibling's pals, will be able to trace ownership in moments. Children can be bloody cruel, and remarkably sharp-eyed when it comes to quality and desirable branded goods. Make sure your kids have a party line: the smart comeback ready in case someone tries to bully them. 'We're fighting climate change' or 'we're protesting against slave labour', say. It might not be completely effective, but it beats having to admit it's all you can afford when you are eight. Keep an eye on them and make sure they feel able to approach you if they are having a tough time with other children. Some schools are excellent at stamping out bullying, others try to ignore it. Conversely, some children are only too happy to inherit much-envied items from admired older siblings, cousins and family friends, but it never hurts to be aware that some children can have mixed feelings about wearing 'cast-offs'.

Not a word of this is to suggest that children need, or should be given, the pricey stuff – they shouldn't. It's good that they learn about basic finance and affordability, but just be aware in case it becomes an issue.

Making things last

Having railed against the indignity of having to wear clothes that were too big myself, it is undeniably wise to buy on the big side when you can: one of my sons grew a foot in height in under a year, and he isn't the only one. Shoes, especially, need to have ample room for growing toes, so it may prove sensible to buy budget shoes regularly than to make the expensive ones last all year.

This is where being handy with a needle and thread comes in, as you can keep good stuff looking good for far longer, or at least until they grow out of things. Ensure you clean trainers and polish school shoes. Even better, teach your children to do it themselves (don't get too excited, though: they rarely show even the slightest interest in doing it), and keep an eye out for the branded items for sale online on sites like eBay, which might just need a little TLC to bring them back to life.

I never buy new shoes for myself and have never had a problem with second-hand ones. To be quite certain, I spray the inside liberally with the aerosol disinfectant and leave them to sit for a day before I wear them. I am also scrupulous about polishing my work shoes regularly to keep them waterproof, and always store them on shoe trees so they keep their shape. Most often I wear rubber-soled comfortable flats, which unfortunately cannot be re-soled, but, for ordinary shoes, reheeling is usually worth it. It is becoming fairly expensive to have them done, however, so if your shoes are from Primark, it may not prove economical, but you can buy DIY stick-on soles and heels online for far less than a good cobbler will charge. Or, if you've invested in a really good-quality pair, either new or second-hand, consider taking them to a cobbler to have an extra layer of thin rubber applied to the ball of the foot and heel, which will protect the shoe and prevent the soles wearing away too quickly, saving money long term. However, with regular maintenance, a pair of good leather shoes should last for years (and it's generally cheaper to address a problem promptly than wait until it gets really bad, when the shoes may be beyond saving). Remember Sam Vimes! (see p. 155)

Household stuff

Check if your area has what's sometimes called a 'library of things'. So much stuff we buy is only used a few times a year (hedge trimmers, carpet cleaners, leaf vacuums, etc.) and borrowing saves not just money but space. If there isn't one nearby, see if you can pool 'stuff' with friends and neighbours rather than each buy all the things. See if there are community groups on Facebook and enquire about loaning someone your lawnmower in exchange for a loan of their leaf shredder.

In my opinion, it often pays to buy more expensive things – sofas, carpets, curtains, etc. – in a neutral style and colour. Fashions in home décor change quickly, so a canny approach is to find a style you like that isn't too extreme or fashion forward, then use accessories to switch things up. If you must paint walls black, then use lining paper first so you can remove it easily, rather than have to apply a dozen layers of undercoat to counteract all that pigment. When, in five years' time, you are trying to strip or cover the matte black doors and skirtings you've seen and copied, you may not remember how much you loved them once and will, without doubt, furiously vow not to make the same mistake again. I assure you the fad for dark paint and/or heavy patterns goes out of fashion before you know it, and having home décor that you can quickly and cheaply update is a great way to stop yourself getting bored and spendy in John Lewis, in my experience. Better to buy new cushion covers than new sofas! Even better, learn to make your own cushion covers from remnants.

If you need new furniture, again, buy second-hand, or go to places like Ikea for things you don't need to last for ever. Like cars, furniture loses its value the second it leaves the shop. A sofa costing several thousand brand new will often sell for several hundred second-hand. It always amazes me how often people invest vast sums of money into curtains, a sofa and all the accessories, only to get bored of the colour scheme and change the lot just a few years later. If you are cautious about buying from eBay or from online selling groups, then see if any of the charity shops nearby sell furniture. There is a British Heart Foundation near us and they are extremely picky about the standards of the furniture they accept, and for a small fee they will even deliver locally. Basic reupholstery is often not as difficult as you would think too: making loose covers requires some sewing skill and a machine (and patience), but re-covering dining-chair seats is easy and requires few tools. You may not be confident enough to make loose covers, but if the existing ones are a linen or cotton mix, you could perhaps dye them? That said, results can vary here: sometimes they look fabulous but be aware that very often stains do *not* dye well, so be reasonable in your expectations.

Christmas and birthdays

Special events are always a challenge for those trying to save money. In many ways it's easier just to announce to everyone you aren't doing presents and be done with it, but you do tend to feel awfully like Scrooge, and then, two days before Christmas, it's all too easy to cave in and end up spending a fortune. It's better to think carefully and avoid the embarrassment of unequal gifts by announcing well in advance you are only giving token gifts this year, say, then come up with small thoughtful gifts for those who matter. Charity shops 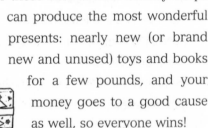 can produce the most wonderful presents: nearly new (or brand new and unused) toys and books for a few pounds, and your money goes to a good cause as well, so everyone wins!

Don't discount charity shops for adult gifts either. One of my clients bought a lot of lovely china mugs, filled them with tea bags, chocolate and other small snacks, then wrapped each mug in cellophane as gifts for those in her office. The added bonus was that it also stopped the year-long bickering about mugs!

Home-made flavoured spirits

Home-made gifts for adults can be simple: if you have access to bramble bushes, blackthorn or damson trees, say, then small bottles of home-made liqueurs are easy, but you need to be organised and start at the end of summer if you're thinking of doing this for Christmas. Pick the fruit when it's available, wash it, then fill empty bottles with the berries, etc. (damsons may need cutting up, as they are quite large, or use a jar), then fill with either gin, brandy or vodka. If you use brandy, then a few cinnamon sticks are a good idea. Add sugar to taste: I only use a few tablespoons per bottle, but some people prefer more (some also suggest only adding sugar later), and use white sugar with vodka and gin, brown for brandy. Stick in a dark cupboard until December (if you remember, give the bottles a shake every now and then). When you are ready to bottle up your booze, find some pretty little bottles or jars and make sure they are spotlessly clean. Empty the contents of the bottles into a jug, using a sieve to hold back the fruit, and check for taste, adding more sugar if needed. Fill and label the bottles. Small bottles are fine: if it looks pretty, it will be well received. I'm not a limoncello lover, so have never bothered to make it, but Skittles or Werther's Original sweets dissolve in vodka and are seriously delicious for those without access to wild fruit (or those who didn't think about this until December).* The only problem I have found with making all these delicious alcoholic concoctions is that you need to sample them before bottling, and as the afternoon goes on, it gets more and more difficult to insert the corks . . . fumes, I expect.†

If you cook, then miniature fruit cakes are often enjoyed: use small baked-bean tins lined in greaseproof to cook a two-person cake and just top with a circle of fondant icing. Don't forget when baking that a smaller volume needs a shorter cooking time (not a bad thing with fruit cake, considering energy prices, as full-sized cakes can take hours to cook). Mine usually work well at 140C for just over an hour.

Older artistically-minded children may enjoy making marzipan petit fours in the shape of fruit. Though I used

---

* 'Dishwasher vodka', where you add various sweets to a bottle of vodka or other spirit, replace the cap tightly, and then run the bottle through a dishwasher cycle, is a particularly rich seam on Mumsnet, I'm told.

† Home-made cordials are nice for teetotal friends, but do check the shelf life. I've had glass bottles with unexpectedly fermenting elder-flower blow up on me before and it's a lethally sharp and sticky mess. For this reason, I'm not suggesting recipes, but there are plenty online.

to make them and then eat them an hour later. Making things like coconut ice or fudge can be a fun activity as well as a nice gift, but inspect hands before they touch anything edible, as it's mortifying spotting a greyish streak in the fudge thirty seconds after you gave some to your neighbour!

Don't be afraid to recycle presents either, but for God's sake keep notes so that you don't return the present to the giver. Scrutinise every inch of it too, as passing on a book your partner lovingly inscribed to you to your boss is horrifying.

For close friends and partners, consider giving and asking for experiences rather than objects, either for things you can provide (dinner for six) or tickets to the theatre, perhaps, or a wine tasting. If you are all past a certain age, the chances are you have everything you want and are keen to avoid unwanted clutter, so a voucher to have your lawn mown in spring, or that border weeded out, is a far more attractive proposition than yet another boxset of toiletries. My grandmother was always pleased to be given tea, and it's only recently I've worked out why – it's a consumable. Rooted cuttings from your garden can also be truly wonderful gifts for the keen gardeners in your life: pot them up nicely and label them with as much information as you have.

Young children

Very young children, in my experience, do not care if a toy is new, and often find too many new things overwhelming anyway. Though it can be difficult if older children don't quite grasp the concept of parental budget. If a belief in Father Christmas is being held on to (like grim death in older kids), try to ensure they expect small token presents from this figure and understand that more substantial ones come from family, who buy them with actual money.*

One of my daughters remembers fondly the huge box of second-hand Barbie stuff we bought her one year. It was a massive box of everything from dolls to furniture (and a lot of shoes, for some reason): it was so much we couldn't hope to sort through it or organise it, so she just got the box all muddled up. It kept her busy for most of January, cost us just under twenty quid, and is hands down the best present she feels she has ever received.

---

* This is also important re comparisons – if 'Father Christmas' brings one of their schoolfriends an Xbox, they may wonder why they were considered so much 'naughtier' and less deserving, and vice versa.

If loving relatives (aka grandparents) arrive with a car-load of presents, you can edit other gifts and ask them if they object to the bounty they bring being staggered over a few days. This does depend on family dynamics, though, as some people get mortally offended, as they want to see the delighted expressions at the gift opening. If they insist every gift is unwrapped there and then, please feel free to hide all others to keep in reserve. I found that, for those under school age, it's best to have a few presents at the usual time, then a present or two at judicious moments throughout the rest of the day, then others staggered over the next week or so. If other family members are considerably richer than you (please say that in Harry Enfield's Birmingham accent or the joke falls flat), perhaps you can steer them towards buying the expensive stuff on Christmas and birthday wish lists? And it's well worth encouraging this behaviour (that is, if they genuinely can afford to stump up), by making the children write thank-you notes – on paper with enve-lopes, the whole hog – as well as giving proper thanks and grateful cuddles at the time, if given in person. Be prepared to take on this mantle re expensive presents as and when your children produce grandchildren, should you be so fortunate – you can then lavish things on them (with their parents' permission) in recognition of the role that grandparents play in the rearing of a child.

Older children

Older children, meanwhile, do better with a framework. Many parents nowadays, for example, make it clear their offspring can have a thing to wear of the child's choice, something to play with up to a maximum amount of money, and two small gifts costing up to a fiver. A popular version of this is: 'something you want, something you need, something to wear and something to read'. On the book side of things, please give book tokens. I was a complete bookworm as a child and book tokens meant a few hours in a bookshop carefully selecting my treasure. That alone was a gift. One of my nieces looks set to become a reader too, so I keep an eye out for good second-hand books I think she will enjoy, then send a parcel once or twice a year. She has full permission to pass on those she doesn't like, but I hope she enjoys the sorting through them as much as I do. I also don't worry too much about Christmas, as random book parcels throughout the year, I hope, are more fun.

Gifts of large or particularly expensive items (phones, bikes, tablets, etc.) need to be understood as a substantial gift, with only a few small tokens to be expected on the side. Those large items need not be new, but just check they are up to the usage they will get, as older children may use these things for school and require a degree of functionality. Things such as laptops and tablets need to run fast enough to be up to scratch. Equally, factor in the age and responsibility of the child. One of mine begged for a mobile phone for months and months; we finally gave in and gave her one, all programmed with numbers and a small pay-as-you-go voucher loaded. She lost it five hours later . . .

Most importantly, *never* borrow money to fund a binge of gifts. It does no one any favours, it's too much for children to appreciate and it risks serious issues later in the year. If the roof starts leaking or the car blows up, you will regret the massive loan you blew on stuff that will be mostly forgotten or broken at that point. It's also all too easy to buy too many presents, which is overwhelming and exhausting for children when they are expected to be excited and grateful for hundreds of things. Aim for quality rather than quantity: a few well-chosen gifts have far more impact.

Festive decorations

Holly, ivy, fir boughs – all are very traditional and make attractive decorations, easily had for the effort of cutting them and bringing indoors (but make sure you ask permission of the landowner and don't strip the hedgerows bare!). They also smell fantastic, but keep in mind that they are highly flammable as they dry out, so keep well away from the fireplace and any candles. Try to cut from up high (keep in mind the height of a large dog – the reason for this should be self-explanatory) and leave your bounty in a bucket of water somewhere sheltered, like a porch, for a couple of days to allow any inhabitants time to vacate. If you prefer to have a real tree, remember to saw an inch off the bottom of the trunk just before you bring it inside and ensure it is kept in water.*

Make your own cards rather than buy them. The simplest way is to cut bits – say bells and angels – from last year's cards and stick them on a plain piece of folded card. Or press flowers to glue on: just pick any blooms you fancy in the warmer months and pop them between the pages of an old magazine with a book on top for the rest of the summer, and by the time November comes round, they will be suitably dried and pressed. My grandmother

---

* Last year we swapped out our old metal-and-horseshoe Christmas-tree stand for a solidly-made plastic one, which securely holds around four litres of water. It's made a huge difference to the amount of needles that drop and I've had no problems with water marking the floorboards.

used to make loads of them, then make cards and parcel tags too. Or get artistic. My mother does one or two very simple designs and mass produces. Last year's was a sprig of alder cones fastened onto the card with two punched holes and a bit of red parcel ribbon. Her boss, who's equally artistically minded, made hers from old music paper twisted into an angel shape, which worked brilliantly and made for an excellent tree ornament.

If you choose to do any of these things I've suggested, I find it makes for a better family evening than watching TV, although probably only younger children will join in. And with a bit of luck it passes the idea and the skill on to the next generation. Be prepared for mess, though: it's startling how far the average three-year-old can spread a small dab of glue.

Christmas dinner

Christmas dinner needn't be the most expensive meal of the year. Cook a lovely meal, but there's no need for a turkey, as, if you eat meat, a small chicken is often nicer, and there are some spectacular nut roast recipes online if you don't. You can actually cook much of a roast dinner in a slow cooker, but the main problem is that it won't crisp up. I solved that by getting everything cooked through in the one pot – chicken in first on high, potatoes, etc. in after three hours – doing that the day before, then letting it cool overnight. Then, having carefully taken everything out and spread it out on an oven tray, I pop it all into the oven on high for half an hour on Christmas Day itself. The only issue I had was the wings fell off the chicken and a few potatoes disintegrated. Which reminds me: do make mountains of roast potatoes, if you can. If you haven't got an oven or an air fryer, the pre-made frozen ones come up well when cooked in a frying pan. Heaps of veg and lots of carrots make up for any deficiencies in the centrepiece department, I've always found.

What really matters

More than anything, though, try to remember that for millennia humans have celebrated the turning of the seasons, getting together to thank whatever god they believed in that the new cycle of life was beginning. Be with people to celebrate being alive, to spend time with others telling bad jokes, singing out-of-key carols – it's not about money, truly. Christmas is often the season for the depressed and lonely to be made to feel truly awful, as, between images of happy families and the adverts for expensive consumer luxuries, it highlights both the lack of family and connection and the lack of money for many people. If you're alone, consider volunteering at a soup kitchen or a shelter, or offer to dish up at the local care home: you will have company – company that will be pleased to see you – and you will be useful to others, which always feels good. I have several friends who took off to wash up at the homeless shelter one year as the rest of their family had other plans and they had such a good time they rather resent having to host said family this year.

If your neighbour is alone, ask them round for a drink if you can't stomach them for lunch, or check with elderly relatives to make sure they aren't sat, alone, having not spoken a word to anyone for days. If they live far away, then perhaps check if there are places they could go for a lunch with others. A good tip is to ask in Facebook groups local to them. Take a dinner round to someone who can't get out and spend half an hour chatting, or, if you have a car, offer to drive them to visit a friend or relative (remember to pick them up again, though).

With a little effort, you'll have both the cheapest and the most satisfying Christmas you've ever had.

Cosmetics

Your beauty routine is another area you can save a fortune on. Billions are spent every year promoting various creams and serums, usually by subtly suggesting that you are a human warthog, and that nobody could ever love you without the help of a trolley full of scented beauty aids. I have even heard these products referred to as 'Hope in a Jar' by someone who worked in advertising.

How often have you seen a wonderful advert for some miracle in a gold pot, featuring a flawless actress swearing blind her beauty is down to a lavish application of the product? You know, realistically, that her complexion is probably down to photoshop (in fact, it often says so in very small writing somewhere), but you still want to try it. Then your favourite influencer reviews it and loves it. Next thing you know, you are sixty quid down and have yet another pot of expensive cream, and you feel more than slightly guilty, as that pot now joins the other twenty you've bought, at least two thirds of which you will never touch until they go off and are thrown away. And it's not just your money you are wasting, but the energy and resources that go into producing things that we simply discard unused. Very often a similar item can be bought with virtually identical ingredients but without the expensive marketing, which is what you are really paying for. One very well-known and extortionately priced cream and good old Nivea reputedly have very similar formulations, but one costs hundreds of pounds more than the other. If you think a product might work for you, then try a sample, read the ingredients, and carefully compare it to other products. We have been trained to equate cost with quality, and that is not always true. Read ingredient lists, check active ingredients, and decide if the expensive option is superior – it often isn't.

A lot of people whose opinions I respect swear by the 'first five ingredients' principle, which suggest that only the first five ingredients on any ingredients list will ever be in sufficient quantities to be effective, and that anything after that is present in such low amounts it will have no effect. This isn't always the case, but it's worth keeping in mind.

Decoding ingredients lists

The INCI list stands for the 'International Nomenclature of Cosmetic Ingredients' and it's in place because ingredients in skincare can have different names in different countries, so having an internationally recognised convention eliminates confusion, making it easier to sell products across the globe.

According to INCI, a skincare brand is required to print the ingredients on the packaging in the order of highest to lowest concentration. Once it gets to ingredients that are included at a concentration of 1% or less, they no longer have to be in order. The first ingredient in any skincare product is usually water or aloe (which is mostly made up of water). These often make up 70–95% of the product, which is perfectly acceptable. After that, the next four ingredients are typically included at concentrations of anywhere between 3–5%. After the first five ingredients, you can still find many performance-based active ingredients, along with thickeners, preservatives, fillers and everything else that makes up a skincare product.*

---

* https://blog.reneerouleau.com/understanding-ingredient-percentages/

Understanding how to read an ingredients list critically will help you make a reasonable comparison between products. More important, though, is understanding that ultimately these products only affect the surface layers of skin: they are cosmetics not drugs. Drugs penetrate our body and, as such, undergo extensive testing; cosmetics aren't required to be nearly as far reaching in their tests, as they cannot penetrate further than the epidermis. The minute a face cream penetrates properly, it becomes a drug, and therefore requires expensive testing, and then different, more stringent laws apply. Obviously, manufacturers avoid this by making certain their products only affect the surface of your skin, so be clued up when it comes to advertising, as it's full of insinuations and short on promises. Nothing truly prevents ageing, and even plastic surgeons and dermatologists can only go so far. No matter how much you spend, all you can reasonably expect is to have good skin, not young skin. In fact, the only thing most skin experts insist on is that you wear a sunscreen, so find one you like and use it religiously. Anything else is up to you and purely down to personal preference, as the best you can hope for is looking good for your age. Growing old should be a source of pleasure, because the only way to avoid growing older is to die, and that's no fun at all.

Personally, I bought myself a cheap serum from Lidl and have been topping it up with samples my daughter doesn't get along with. Everything gets put in the bottle and shaken together, and it seems to work just as well no matter what is in there. That said, I am fortunate not to suffer from any specific skin complaints or conditions, such as rosacea or eczema. If you need a richer cream, then look for shea butter or cocoa butter – they are both excellent rich moisturisers and can be had for a fraction of the price of the much-advertised and lauded fancy face creams promoted by actors and supermodels on million-dollar contracts.

Quite a lot of very pleasing lotions and potions can be made at home, and many household ingredients, such as oatmeal, make lovely scrubs. Herbal hair rinses smell wonderful (camomile will brighten blonde hair, while rosemary brings out the lights in a brunette) and one of the most efficient body lotions going is to rub sunflower oil into damp skin. If you want it to smell nice, then add a few drops of essential oil.

DIY

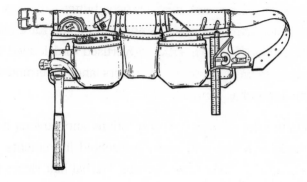

Renovations

This is another area where, with a bit of know-how and elbow grease, you can save a small fortune. Some work *must* be done by a certified tradesperson, though – gas, for example, can only be touched by a certified engineer, mainly because you can blow up the house, risking your own life and others', if it is done incorrectly.

Electrics are often best done by a trained electrician too, but simple electrical jobs are perfectly manageable – fuses, plugs, etc. – but, once again, you can inadvertently cause a lot of damage if you aren't completely sure what you are doing, so proceed with common sense and an excess of caution. You may not be the first DIYer let loose on a particular house, and combining two untrained amateurs can be a recipe for disaster: the professionals test circuits and are aware of common pitfalls. I take things I am unsure about to a repair café we are fortunate to have held monthly at our local town hall – qualified electricians are on hand to test small appliances and will very often replace a connection or a fuse inside, whereas the manufacturer would just insist you replaced it. It's well worth checking if you too have something like this in your area.

Plumbing is more 50/50 on the difficulty scale, but much of it is simple. Changing taps, for example, just requires long arms and a wrench. The problem can arise if you are not careful when doing up joints, as water can do an alarming amount of damage in a very short window of time. I'd be happier doing basic plumbing jobs in a house, as in a flat you risk flooding downstairs if anything goes wrong and your insurance might not pay up if you've been a bit of an idiot. Before you start any plumbing job at all, however, please check isolation valves and stopcocks, making sure they all turn easily so that, in an emergency, you can shut the water off quickly. Things like plumbing in your washing machine are straightforward. Tasks such as putting in a garden tap require a little more work, but compression joints have done away with the need to solder, so once you have the knack, many small repairs are easily done. YouTube videos can teach you almost anything.*

Jobs such as carpentry and decorating can also be done by non-professionals if you're looking to save money, and with a little care and attention you can produce excellent results. I'd recommend going over what you need to do (several times) well in advance so you understand what you are doing, then working out a plan of action and (this is very important) an order of operation. Use dustsheets and do not rush. You will find lots of videos and channels on YouTube of people who have taught themselves all sorts of skills, from plastering to roofing to groundwork

---

* YouTube is full of thousands of videos showing you how to do everything from mending a chair to replacing a roof. Some of these videos are excellent, clear and informative. Others are downright wrong, giving false and sometimes dangerous information. Always read the comments, and always watch several. I personally find it easier to follow from a book rather than watch a video, although watching someone do a job several times is certainly a help.

and paving. It absolutely can be done, but don't charge in on the strength of a two-minute video.

You'll find the discount supermarkets have a wide selection of reasonably priced tools, many of which are fairly essential. These cut-price tools are not robust enough for a professional, but for the home DIYer will be perfectly adequate to start with – as ever, don't go all out and buy expensive kit you may only use once. However, it is true that good tools often make a job much easier and less stressful, so while laying out a hundred quid seems a lot, that's a day's wage for a labourer and will save so much time it is worth it. If you doubt me, try screwing in a 20mm screw by hand, then try using a screwdriver bit in a cordless drill. Multiply the difference by forty screws in a cabinet and you'll understand what I mean.

Always allow yourself time to clear up and put your tools away at the end of a day, as it takes longer than you think and, if you work until exhausted, you will make stupid mistakes.

Painting and decorating

Decorating is very much a job you can learn, as, generally speaking, most of the work is in the preparation. Making absolutely certain the surfaces are clean and filled, then sanded smooth, reaps dividends when you come to paint and paper. Papering is harder than painting, though, so don't try to use expensive wallpaper until you have mastered the art. There is a fashion at present for very dark walls, but fashions change and, at some point in the future, you may want to paint over that dark green wall with pale pink paint. That, of course, as we have discussed, will lead you to question your past choices mightily, as it will take multiple coats (and paint isn't cheap anymore) and may end up looking messy. The answer is to use lining paper: it will leave a nice, smooth and even surface to paint on, and, in five years' time or whenever you're up for a change, you can simply strip off the paper and either repaper or clean and fill the wall and paint on that.

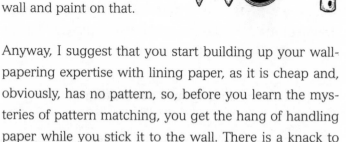

Anyway, I suggest that you start building up your wallpapering expertise with lining paper, as it is cheap and, obviously, has no pattern, so, before you learn the mysteries of pattern matching, you get the hang of handling paper while you stick it to the wall. There is a knack to this, so go slowly, and try not to lose your temper. Then, once you are confident with lining paper, move on to proper wallpaper, starting with something inexpensive in a small room. The loo is an ideal place to start, but it's a small room, as a rule, so you'll need a certain amount of dexterity to get everything looking perfect. However, if you mess it up, it's not the end of the world if you need to start from scratch. Only move on to the high-end stuff once you are certain you can manage it.[*]

A word of warning: if your room is decorated with woodchip wallpaper, be aware it was often used to hold crumbling walls together, and it frequently had numerous coats of paint applied on top too, to make matters worse. You may well find you need to engage a plasterer once you have finally removed the last shred of paper. Brown-varnished anaglypta is much the same, but you see it less and less these days, as most of it has been removed since it went out of fashion many decades ago.

Likewise Artex ceilings in pretty swirly patterns (or just the lumpy ones): Artex was a solution for cracks and

---

[*] A good tip is to try to remember to write under the very last sheet of paper how many rolls of what kind (the dimensions, etc.) of paper it took. It means that when you – or the next person – pull the paper down again, you can double check you have enough before you start the next time you do it!

crumbling plasterwork, so be careful if you decide to remove it. Many of these ceilings also contain asbestos, so check before you remove anything. It is possible to steam it off, but the best suggestion is to plaster over it. Even if you like a textured ceiling, be aware they are virtually impossible to match up should you need to do a repair, and can be surprisingly difficult to paint as well. If that wasn't enough, they are also really difficult to clean, as they hang on to cobwebs like grim death. As you may have guessed, I'm not a fan.

When decorating, *always* use dustsheets. When I say that preparation is the way to get good results, that includes readying the space. Mask with tape, use dustsheets, and never leave open tins of paint where you can trip over one. And, just as with any other DIY, it's key to make sure you leave enough time at the end of the session to clean up properly.

When you have finished, decant any leftover paint in a tin (assuming the tin isn't mostly full) into a glass coffee jar and label it clearly with the room you painted, the name, brand and colour code of the paint and any other information you may think you will need. This should make the occasional touch-up easy and saves accumulating too many bulky and nearly empty paint tins.

Other home improvements

A garden renovation project can be rewarding, and obviously can save thousands. Laying a patio is a fairly simple job, but, as ever, you need to be very careful to do it properly, and paving slabs are heavy. Wear gloves and make sure you are capable of lifting them into place before you start.

Simple home repair jobs and quick revamps of your existing furniture are well worth mastering too. The term 'upcycle' makes me cringe slightly, as I've seen so much furniture smothered in lumpy chalk paint with smudgy mottoes stencilled on it I could cry. Done well, though, it's an ingenious way to tart up a room. Just as preparation is the key to making a room look Instagram-worthy, so it is with furniture. Ensure everything is cleaned, sanded and all minor repairs done before you paint. Chalk paint is very fashionable but it isn't easy to clean; even when carefully waxed, stains tend to soak in. Please try not to paint good antique furniture either – there was a lot of nice stuff painted with white gloss in the 70s, then a lot of time spent in the 80s trying to remove the gloss paint as antique prices had risen significantly. Far safer to start with things you don't care about ruining. If things go wrong, you can throw them away. I have, however, seen some spectacular things done with a little expensive wallpaper and paint to finish – even gold leaf used to transform cheap junkshop finds – but just refinishing and replacing hardware can produce a huge improvement. I have a dresser I store china in (and on), for example: it was a rather nasty 80s-orange pine one and looked tired and dated, so I painted it with stone-coloured eggshell paint (it's a more robust finish than chalk paint) and replaced the handles while leaving the shelves and top plain wood. Total cost of £15 for paint, handles and sand-paper, as I already had the brushes. It now looks virtually identical to one sold for nearly £600.

Make your own

I'm also lumping making your own gear in this section. I started wild swimming in lockdown, and rather fancied a Dryrobe, which were retailing for well over a hundred pounds at the time. Instead I made my own – it was awk-ward, although not terribly difficult. But while finding out about such arcane subjects as ripstop nylon, I discovered an entire community on Reddit of people who make their own gear. Rucksacks, tents, garden furniture – almost anything can be made at home. Obviously a lot of this requires specialist equipment, and it's not always practical or economical to buy a pile of stuff just to make a few items, but it's always worth investigating what you can do, especially if you are having trouble finding something you need. I want a thick, robust cover for my bike, for example. Most are quite lightweight fabric, aren't terribly waterproof and tear if they get caught up on the chain mechanism. This winter I will take a few measurements and make myself a robust and suitably waterproof one, which, hopefully, will last me several years. Once you get the bug for making stuff, it's a practical hobby in itself, as not only does it prevent you just mindlessly buying things, it also fills quite a bit of free time. If you are particularly talented, it could even segue into a nice little earner, but more about that in the next chapter.

Ideas for repurposing jumpers

Now for those old jumpers past their best I mentioned earlier (or hoodies and sweatshirts). Lay each jumper flat and cut both the front and the back into two large rectangles – avoid the seams and the neckline. These rectangles can be sewn together to make a knee rug, or made into a couple of hot water bottle covers, or, if made from cotton, effective dusters. Cut each arm off too and save the offcuts – seams, collars, cuffs, etc. – to stuff something like a draught excluder. The first eight inches of each sleeve, meanwhile, can be adapted into wrist warmers: make a hole in the seam for your thumb to go through, then sew to fit snugly over your wrists and hem neatly. The rest of the sleeve can either be cut into another rectangle for repurposing, or used to make either ankle warmers or leg warmers. Or, if the sleeves are quite baggy, you can sew up one end neatly and make a bag hat!

WAYS OF MAKING EXTRA MONEY

Side hustles – dos and don'ts

The easiest way to earn a bit of spare cash is by selling stuff you no longer want or need. I found larger, heavier stuff is easier to sell on Facebook Marketplace, as there are no selling fees and you want people to collect, although eBay will sort by nearest first, which is handy. I'm not sure if you can post a wardrobe, but probably not (though I've heard that people who habitually buy second-hand furniture online often use courier companies who specialise in such jobs and factor the cost in when buying). Don't just stick with eBay, though, as there are plenty of other online selling platforms: Gumtree, Vinted, and even old-school car boot sales. There are a lot of options out there, so work out what's best for what you're looking to sell.

Once you've worked out what site is best for what you have in mind, have a browse through what similar items to yours are fetching on that particular platform, then factor in the selling fees, and weigh your item to be certain you charge the correct postage too! Make sure you take good clear pictures, be unflinchingly honest about any flaws and be realistic about what the item will fetch. I usually look up only what something might sell for at auction, as it's all very well asking a high price for something but it might take months to sell, incurring several lots of fees. Often, if you auction something starting on the low side of its value, it will net you a higher sale price, but there are no guarantees, so don't start an auction at 99p if you aren't prepared to sell for that. Some people make a comfortable amount by buying stuff at jumble sales and charity shops and reselling on eBay, but I have never had any luck at all doing that. However, if you do want to give it a go, it seems wisest to pick a specialist area – vintage jeans or cookware, say – then you can focus on finding what you know will sell and will quickly get a feel for how to price it and how to present it. Do not, however, fall in love with half of your stock and decide to keep it!

Pitfalls

I've heard it said that the fastest way to make a small fortune is to start with a large one and invest. And I have seen a worrying number of people trying to sell investment schemes on TikTok, often claiming to get people to become what are known as 'retail traders'. A retail trader is someone who buys and sells stocks and shares for themselves. To start with, between 70–97% of retail traders lose money over the course of a year, so the likelihood of this sort of scheme making you a fortune is remote – a salient fact they are supposed to tell you about but very often don't as they then hurriedly rush through the bit about stocks going down as well as up. All these chiselled-jawed chaps are trying to make money by getting commission from *you*, not from investing money in stocks and shares, you see. They virtually always try to persuade you that property is a poor investment, and they usually show themselves driving an expensive car, then burble on about how you too can be wealthy. They always seem to get up at 4am and go to the gym, drink some weird green stuff for breakfast and have what they assume are aspirational lifestyles. It all sounds exhausting, and it's highly unlikely they actually stick to the routine they espouse as the whole schtick is for you to try and emulate them by buying what they are selling, and they are *always* selling something.

Very often it's a training course to learn retail trading, or it is cryptocurrency of some sort. If you have a huge hole in your finances, then the very worst thing to do is start gambling, and these investment schemes *are* gambling. Yes, some people have made a small fortune, but then some people have also won the lottery and we have definite odds for that: 14,000,000 to 1. How they make *their* money is by parting you from yours, so beware!

A nice problem to have – spare cash

If you're fortunate enough to have a surplus of cash, then put it in the bank – while it will be affected by inflation, at least it won't evaporate completely. Instant access savings accounts rarely offer much in the way of interest, but things such as fixed term bonds offer a better deal, though they require you to put a certain amount of cash into an account with no access for a fixed term, often a year. At the end of that year you can access this money plus the interest. Check, of course, that the scheme is insured with the FSCS (Financial Services Compensation Scheme) and make sure that you don't invest more than the scheme is covering you for.

If you have enough money to start buying land and property, I'm fairly sure you wouldn't have bought this book in the first place, but as long as you don't have an expensive mortgage in place to buy it, land and property can be a fairly safe bet. However, if there's a crash, it's possible to find yourself in negative equity, where you owe more than the property is worth. In that instance, you can either sell at a loss or continue to pay the mortgage and hope things improve – in other words, *never* overextend yourself. The global crash in 2008 was caused by banks lending too much money to people who couldn't really afford it, and this pushed up house prices. When those house prices came down and people defaulted on their mortgages, it crashed the global economy. So while it may seem annoying that the rules are stringent when you're trying to get a loan or mortgage, those rules are there to protect everyone involved.

Making a hobby a business

Sometimes a small business can provide a handy income, but no matter what you do, make certain you are doing it properly. I know too many people who have fallen foul of regulations or accounting rules. The other thing is pricing, and there is a formula for this.

I make a doodah – let's call it X: it costs me £10 to make X, and I can make 10 X a day. I have to sell X for enough money to cover my costs as a business and make enough profit to live on. If I sold each X for £15, I would make £50 a day after costs, and that's not enough money to live on even if I didn't have things like advertising and postage and packing as well. So assuming my costs are about £10 a day for advertising, and it's £4 an X doodah for postage (£40 a day), and I need to earn at least £100 a day to live, that would mean my doodah would have to sell for £25 a piece. Is that more than it is worth? Or is it too little? Before you sell anything, you must ensure it is worth it, as that thing needs to earn you a living. That means costing out absolutely everything, every staple, every sheet of paper and envelope, the heating, the rent, etc. You have to be brutally realistic.

This is why stuff such as cake making and those insanely clever crafts rarely make money – the time and effort it takes to make these works of art makes them very expensive, and while they are undoubtedly worth it, many people are unwilling to spend several hundred pounds on a cake or thousands of pounds on a quilt. Obviously, some people do, but it is a hard market to break into.

It might be easier to see if you can pick up another part-time job. Bar work is harder than you think, but it works really well as a money saver, because, as I found out, your social life will vanish, largely because you will be expected to work weekends, as obviously that is when a bar or a pub is busiest. That said, you do get to spend time at the pub, and in a smaller local venue, it can be an enjoyably sociable job. However, if you work behind a bar, be aware you cannot drink. Once upon a time it used to be considered a perk of the trade, and many pub landlords, I'm sorry to say, had serious alcohol issues, but those days are long gone. In general, hospitality work is really tiring too, as most of the time you are running around, on your feet non-stop, and very often you aren't home until gone midnight.

The drawbacks of the hospitality industry are why I got into cleaning as a full-time career. I had been doing bar and kitchen work as a back-up to being self-employed in various craft-based ventures, but as my children grew older, the late nights became difficult. I picked up a few cleaning jobs instead to fill a gap. Then things grew until cleaning filled all the time I had.

I have been lucky in being able to pick up work fairly quickly, although I must say I virtually never refuse any paid work: I'm always worried that, if I refuse, I won't be asked again. Doing multiple jobs is exhausting, and you must be reliable. Plus, if you are self-employed, you do not get paid if you are ill or take a vacation. You cannot sack yourself, however, so if you have a spread of clients, you should have a fairly regular income, as you rarely lose every client at once. It's possible, though: if you behave atrociously with one client, word will get out and the others can and will drop you fast!

I've also, clearly, been lucky with social media, but that is luck in the extreme rather than any considered decision and *not* a reliable suggestion. I might also point out that it doesn't pay millions. Obviously, we all know influencers who have supposedly made a fortune, but, for most of us, it's a part-time job. We do it for pleasure, and I'd be lying if I said vanity didn't come into it!

But there are all sorts of odd things people sign up for – one friend works as an extra in various films; the pay isn't bad, the catering truck is brilliant, and his left leg appears in at least one film I've seen. My wonderful editor, Anna, pointed out cashback websites too, so I trotted off and had a look. It reminded me of how, when I first started using the internet, I filled in lots of surveys to get an M&S gift voucher. It came in handy at the time as I really needed new pants (and the ones I bought way back then only died about two years ago). However, a word of warning here: bear in mind that all of these schemes exist because they drive spending. Even my innocuous Marks and Sparks voucher took me into a shop I would not normally have used and, once in, I used my voucher and then went on to spend a few extra pounds I wouldn't have otherwise. If you use a cashback scheme, be vigilant about not being tempted to start spending that little bit extra. If they give you back money on something you would have bought no matter what, they are a great idea, but if you find you can't help overspending, it's best to ignore them.

Dog walking, gardening, babysitting, waitressing/waitering – the list of odds and ends you can top the coffers up with is quite long, but make sure you use your head and check out any relevant rules and regulations, as well as things such as insurance. Taking your grandmother's Labrador out for a stroll on Sunday is very different to walking five pedigree Salukis twice a day, so you'd almost certainly want insurance, which needs to be factored in as a cost.

Of course, it's wonderful to think you can make money doing what you love – turning a much-loved hobby into an income stream – but the downside is that you can quickly lose the love you have for anything if you start relying on it for money.

Oh, and pay your tax, and your national insurance too! You can get into a lot of trouble if you avoid tax, so make sure it's all above board. And national insurance contributions are vital as old age approaches, as they relate to whether or not you can claim a state pension.

CONCLUSION

I find that a lot about saving money is down to mindset: when times get tough, you can either struggle along buying the cheapest version of your current lifestyle and spend your life feeling deprived, or you can decide you have had enough of the brainwashing and disconnect. As I have mentioned several times in this book, from birth we are bombarded with advertising of all sorts espousing resource-heavy lifestyles. The pictures you see on Instagram and in the glossy interiors magazines have been curated to the nth degree: stylists spend hours arranging the contents of a room so it photo-graphs perfectly. They add all sorts of accessories (neatly priced out in the captions) and the room you see bears no resemblance to the same room two weeks later on a rainy Friday. Personally, I'm always astounded, and not a little annoyed, that the pictures of country self-sufficiency don't reveal the sheer volume of mud involved!

Like it or not we live in a capitalist society, and so much of what we see about us is a fiction designed to part us from our money. That peaceful little cabin we daydream about is simply that: a dream. The reality is an entirely different prospect, with maybe a small amount of peace and tranquillity, but a hefty dose of backbreaking work. We can, though, adjust our way of thinking to ensure we don't waste our hard-earned money on things that don't actually benefit us all that much, instead directing our spending to things that enrich our lives in measurable ways.

All of us fantasise about spending more time with our pets, our children, our significant other, but, in reality, we are so exhausted trying to keep up with the perfect fam-ilies we see pictured online we lose touch with what that actually means. Humans, as a rule, need to feel part of a group; we need interaction and connection much more than expensive bits of plastic. It's entirely possible to live a pleasant and comfortable life by making a few simple but fundamental changes to how you attend to your needs. Think of what you are trying to achieve as the end point and recognise that, very often, you can get there far more easily and directly than you would if you adopted the consumer solution. Quite a few of the things I mention in this book take a bit more time than the alternative, but so does shopping! And, frankly, spending a Saturday making sweets and Christmas cards with the children rather than battling the crowds in the town centre sounds far more appealing.

But whatever you choose, and however you decide to navigate the current and any future crises, I hope I have opened your eyes a little and made you feel you have options. We are all worth more than the sum of our spending power. After all, our bank balances are the least interesting things about every single one of us!

Acknowledgements

Once again, I owe a huge amount to the wonderful team at Headline, with special mentions to Anna Steadman and Anna Hervé. Their giving me the chance to witter on again was an absolute joy; you have enriched my life immeasurably.

To my siblings, who basically wrote the bit about camping: you're all weird, but I love you anyway . . . as long as you never make me sleep in a tent ever again.

To my followers, who started this whole affair: I hope I have taught you a few useful tips, but thank you so very much for the chance.

And, finally, to baby Arthur, who made an unscheduled early appearance just as this book was going off to be typeset: I wish you a most satisfying life.

Index

addiction 49–50
advertising
    avoiding 4–5
    clothes 154–5
    cosmetics 178, 181
    excess product usage 102–3
    pressure to consume 150–1,
        205–6
ageing 181
air flow 78–80, 83, 84, 92–3
air fryers 112–13
alcohol 120
allotments 142–4

bacon 7, 136–7
bank accounts 13
banking apps 53
bar work 201–2
batch cooking 107, 119
baths 95–6
bedrooms 77–8
bicarbonate of soda 87

bicycles 33–5
bills 13–15
birthdays 166–73
blanching vegetables 108
blankets and rugs 75, 76–7
books 29, 172
bread/breadcrumbs 7, 135,
        140–1
budgeting
    categorising current
        spending 9–11
    cutting out non-essentials
        11–13
    living within your income
        16
    loans 17
    money management 13, 15
    monthly spending money
        18–19
    savings 20–1
    treats 12–13
bulk buying 26, 122–3

bus passes 33
buy now, pay later schemes
   16–17

camping 39–42
capitalism 206
car boot sales 194
carbon monoxide alarms 61
carpentry 185
carrots 7
cars
   costs 34, 35
   fuel 32
   lift sharing 32
   loans 17
   type 35–6
   urban/rural options 32
cash 16, 150
cashback schemes 203
cavity wall insulation 59
cement render 82
change, saving it 52–3
charity shops 29–30, 166
children
   camping 41
   clothes 158–62
   presents 28–9, 170–3
   socialising 43–4
   talking about finances 74
   walking 31

Christmas
   dealing with loneliness
      176–7
   decorations 173–5
   dinner 175–6
   gifts 166–73
chutneys 123
clanger 136–7
cleaning
   clothes 87–92
   earning money 202
   household 85–7
   yourself 93–103
clothes
   advertising 154–5
   altering and making 157
   children 158–62
   cleaning 87–92
   fast fashion 154, 155
   history 153–4
   keeping warm 74–7
   mending 88, 155–6
   second-hand 157–8, 160–1
   tailored 88
clubs and groups 46–7
coaches 36–7
community food-sharing
      groups 125
comparison websites 14
compost 144

condensation 62, 64, 78, 81

conkers 86

consumerism 4, 23–5, 149–50, 151, 205–6

cooking
air fryers 112–13
batch cooking 107, 119
cake 139–40
cheap meals 129–30
Christmas dinner 175–6
clanger 136–7
cost versus time 127
gifts 168–9
hay box 115
microwave ovens 111–12, 132
multi-purpose cookers 113–14
pressure cookers 114–15
puddings 138–9, 141
from scratch 127–9
slow cookers 111
stretching ingredients 128–9, 130–2
stuffed pancakes 134–5

cosmetics 178–82

cost-of-living crisis 1

credit cards 16, 50, 150

credit ratings 21

cryptocurrency 198

curtains 62, 65–6

cycling 33–5

damp
avoidance 78–80
types 80–3

debts 49–51

decorating 186–9

decorations, Christmas 173–5

dehumidifiers 79–80, 84, 92

Dickens, Charles 16

dieting 12

'dishwasher vodka' 168n

DIY 183–93

doors, adjusting for draughts 65–6

dopamine hit 4

draughts 64–6

drinks 120, 167–8

electrics 184

emergency savings 51

energy
estimating usage 69–70
house energy performance 55–6
used everywhere 3
see also heating; utility bills

environment, reducing
consumption 5
envy 4
exercise
cycling 34
walking 30–1

fast fashion 154, 155
fireplaces 70–2
floor types and heating 60–1
food
Christmas dinner 175–6
community sharing groups
125
entertaining 44
food banks 125, 126–7
homemade meal deals
19–20
meal planning 107, 118–19
nutrition 132–3
preserving 123–5
shopping 106, 117–18, 120–1
treats and takeaways 13
'value-added' products 128
variety 131
veganism/vegetarianism
116, 132–3
waste 133–6
see also cooking
freezers 106–10

frugality 5–6, 24
furniture 164–5, 190–1

gambling 49–50, 198
gifts 166–73, 174–5
growing vegetables 142–7
gutters 81
gym memberships 96

hair washing 98–100
hand washing 98
hay box cooking 115
heating
central heating versus
portable heaters
66–7
costs 57–61
draughts 64–6
fireplaces 70–2
floor types 60–1
general principles 72–4
warm banks 68–9
windows 61–4
hobbies
cutting spending 29–30
earning money with 200–1,
204
holidays 37–42, 51–2
home furnishings 164–5
hospitality work 201–2

hot water bottles 75, 77

house swaps 38

household hygiene 85–7

housing, renting 21, 81

INCI list 180

income, living within 16

influencers 5, 27, 178

insulation 59–60, 66

insurance 14–15, 204

interest rates 50–1

investments 197–8

jam 123

jobs, part-time 201–4

jumpers, repurposing 75, 192–3

knitting 30

landlords 81

language and positivity 5

lemons 87

libraries

   books 29

   of things 163–4

loans 17, 173

marketing emails 27

meal planning 107, 118–19

microbiome 98

microwave ovens 111–12, 132

mildew 83–4

mindset 205

money as a product 53–4

mortgages 50–1, 199–200

mothballs 88–9

mould 79, 83–4

needs versus wants 54, 150–1

negative equity 199

nutrition 132–3

painting 186–9

pancakes, savoury stuffed 134–5

patios 190

payments, contactless versus cash 18–19, 150

pets 75–6

pleasure, budgeting for 12–13

plumbing 184–5

pointing (between bricks) 82

poverty 2

presents 166–73, 174–5

preserving food 123–5

pressure cookers 114–15

puddings 138–9, 141

queen of puddings 141

rationing 122, 133

recycling, selling items 195–7

render 82

renovations 183–6

renting homes

    damp 81

    moving expenses 21

renting white goods 21

retail traders 197–8

retailer tricks 25–6, 121, 149–50

Russell, Ann

    background 6

    mother 5, 7

sale prices 27

sandwiches, homemade 19–20

savings 20–1, 51–4, 198–9

school run 31–2

'scrap roast' 135

second-hand items 24, 29–30, 40, 151–2, 157–8, 160–1, 165

self-employment 202

selling items 195–8

shampoo 99

Shelter 81

shoes 162–3

shopping

    avoiding impulse buys 25–6

    bulk buying 26, 122–3

cashback schemes 203

cosmetics 178–82

dopamine hit 4

food 106, 117–18, 120–1

furniture 164–5

gifts 166–73

heavy items 26, 28

online 26–7

planning beforehand 152–3

society pressure to consume 23–5, 149–50, 151

see also clothes

short-date-coded foods 117–18

showering 94–5, 96

slow cookers 111

soap 99–101

social media

    earning money 202–3

    influencers 5, 27, 178, 202–3

    marketing 26–7

    perfection images 25, 206

socialising 42–7

soda crystals 28, 101–2

soup 129–30

spirits, home-made flavoured 167–8

staycations 37

StepChange.org 49

strip washing 96–7

subscriptions 11

sunscreens 181

takeaways 13
tax 204
tools 164, 186
toothpaste 102–3
trains 36–7
transport
    cycling 33–5
    public 32, 33
    trains and coaches 36–7
    walking 31–3
    see also cars
treats, budgeting for 12–13

upcycling 190
utility bills 13–15, 56–7, 67–8,
    69–70

veganism/vegetarianism 116,
    132–3

vegetables
    blanching 108
    cold storage 110
    homegrown 142–7
    seasonality 131
ventilation 78–80, 83, 84, 92–3
vinegar 86–7, 90
vitamins 133
volunteering 45–6, 177

walking 31–3
wallpapering 187–8
wants versus needs 54, 150–1
wartime advice 122, 123
washing
    clothes 89–90
    yourself 93–103
white goods, renting 21
Wilde, Oscar 2
windows 57, 61–4, 81